R. Gupta's®

POPULAR

ARITHMETIC

MULTIPLE CHOICE QUESTIONS

Useful for

ALL COMPETITIVE EXAMINATIONS

Ramesh Publishing House, New Delhi

Published by
O.P. Gupta *for* Ramesh Publishing House

Admin. Office
12-H, New Daryaganj Road, Opp. Officers' Mess,
New Delhi-110002 ① 23261567, 23275224, 23275124

E-mail: info@rameshpublishinghouse.com
Website: www.rameshpublishinghouse.com

Showroom
● Balaji Market, Nai Sarak, Delhi-6 ① 23253720, 23282525
● 4457, Nai Sarak, Delhi-6, ① 23918938

Book Code: R-382

ISBN: 978-81-7812-693-7

HSN Code: 49011010

CONTENT

R. Gupta's®
USEFUL INTELLIGENCE/REASONING/QUIZ BOOKS

Book Name	Code	Price (₹)
Reasoning Skills	R-1640	295
All About Reasoning (Verbal & Non-Verbal)	R-768	495
रीजनिंग टेस्ट (भाषिक एवं अभाषिक)	R-807	540
All About Reasoning (Verbal)	R-296	345
रीजनिंग टेस्ट (भाषिक)	R-785	295
All About Reasoning (Non-Verbal)	R-767	240
रीजनिंग टेस्ट (अभाषिक)	R-805	210
Test of Reasoning Ability	R-835	110
Logical and Analytical Reasoning	R-273	140
बौद्धिक एवं तर्कशक्ति परीक्षा (भाषिक एवं अभाषिक)	R-181	120
Test of Non-Verbal Reasoning	R-300	130
Mental Ability Test	R-784	190
General Intelligence Test/Mental Ability Test	R-42	150
सामान्य बुद्धिमत्ता परीक्षण/मानसिक योग्यता परीक्षा	R-513	120
Digest for SSB Interviews & Psycho-Intelligence Tests	R-186	295
World Quiz Book	R-555	150
India Quiz Book	R-556	120
Intelligence Quiz Book-1	R-646	70
Intelligence Quiz Book-2	R-647	70
Religion, Mythology & Culture Quiz Book	R-700	40
Geography Quiz Book	R-723	55
Junior English Quiz Book	R-764	50
Senior English Quiz Book	R-765	70

Ramesh Publishing House

12-H, New Daryaganj Road, Opp. Officers' Mess, Delhi-110002
For Online Shopping: www.rameshpublishinghouse.com

1908

1

NUMBER SYSTEM

1. The greatest number of 5 digits formed with the digits 6, 9, 0, 2 and 1 is:
   A. 10926
   B. 69201
   C. 96210
   D. 29610

2. The greatest prime number of two digits is:
   A. 93
   B. 99
   C. 89
   D. 97

3. The difference between the greatest number of four digits and the smallest number of five digits is:
   A. 1
   B. 11
   C. 1111
   D. 8999

4. What is the difference between the place values of two 2's in 23200?
   A. 0
   B. 198
   C. 1980
   D. 19800

5. What is the number which when divided by 15, gives a quotient 15 and a remainder 5?
   A. 80
   B. 230
   C. 220
   D. 90

6. How many prime numbers are there between 1 to 100?
   A. 22
   B. 18
   C. 25
   D. 24

7. Difference between the squares of two consecutive numbers is 23. These numbers are:
   A. 13, 14
   B. 8, 9
   C. 12, 13
   D. 11, 12

8. Which of the following is the smallest 4 digit number that can be formed by using the digits 0, 1, 2, and 3?
   A. 0123
   B. 1023
   C. 1203
   D. 1230

9. Find the sum of all the first-15 odd natural numbers.
   A. 200
   B. 215
   C. 225
   D. 235

10. A number having 2, 3 and 7 as a prime factor is:
    A. 52
    B. 42
    C. 32
    D. 72

11. In the following which is the greatest number?
    A. $(4)^2$
    B. $[(2 + 2)^2]^2$
    C. $(2 \times 2 \times 2)^2$
    D. $(2 + 2 + 2)^2$

12. The product of two prime numbers is:
    A. Odd number
    B. Even number
    C. Prime number
    D. Composite number

13. The next number in the sequence 1, 7, 3, 9, 5, 11, ... is:
    A. 7
    B. 13
    C. 15
    D. 17

14. Which of the following is not a prime number:

A. 79   B. 83

C. 87   D. 97

15. Think of a number, divide it by 9 and add 9 to it, if the result is 27, the number is:

A. 18   B. 162

C. 21   D. 100

16. The number which when added to itself 10 times gives 264, the number is:

A. 20   B. 22

C. 26   D. 24

17. Ram eats 8 bananas in the morning, 5 in the afternoon and 2 in the evening. How many dozens of bananas does he eat in a day.

A. $1\frac{1}{4}$ B. $\frac{1}{4}$

C. $\frac{3}{13}$ D. $14\frac{17}{30}$

18. The sum of two numbers is 25 and the difference of their square is 75. Find the difference between the numbers.

A. 2   B. 3

C. 4   D. 5

19. John ranks twenty first in a class of fifty-one. What is his rank from the last?

A. 31   B. 30

C. 17   D. 21

20. If "+" means 'multiplied by',

"−" means 'divided by',

"×" means 'plus',

"÷" means 'minus', then

$(18 + 10 \times 20) - 8 \div 6 = ?$

A. 35   B. 92

C. 26   D. 19

ANSWERS

1	2	3	4	5	6	7	8	9	10
C	D	A	D	B	C	D	B	C	B

11	12	13	14	15	16	17	18	19	20
B	D	A	C	B	D	A	B	A	D

EXPLANATORY ANSWERS

1. The greatest number of five digits formed by the digits 6, 9, 0, 2 and 1

$$= 96210.$$

2. 97 is the greatest prime number of two digits.

3. Smallest number of five digits

$$= 10000$$

Greatest number of four digits

$$= 9999$$

Difference $= 10000 - 9999 = 1.$

4. Place value of 2 in 23200

$$= 20000$$

Place value of 2 = 200

Difference $= 20000 - 200 = 19800$

5. Quotient = 15, divisor = 15 and remainder = 5

Dividend = Quotient × divisor

$$+ \text{ remainder}$$

$= 15 \times 15 + 5 = 225 + 5 = 230$

Hence, the number = 230

6. There are 25 prime numbers between 1 to 100.

7. Let two consecutive numbers are x and $x + 1$.

According to the question,

$$(x + 1)^2 - (x)^2 = 23$$
$$\Rightarrow \quad x^2 + 2x + 1 - x^2 = 23$$
$$\Rightarrow \quad 2x + 1 = 23$$
$$\Rightarrow \quad 2x = 22$$
$$\Rightarrow \quad x = 11$$

$\therefore$ Numbers are 11 and 12.

8. 1023 is the smallest 4 digit number that can be formed by using the digits 0, 1, 2 and 3.

9. The sum of first-n odd natural numbers $= n^2$

$\therefore$ Sum of first-15 odd natural numbers $= (15)^2 = 225$.

10. $\because$ 2, 3, 7 are the prime factors of the number

$\therefore$ number $= 2 \times 3 \times 7 = 42$.

11.
$$(4)^2 = 4 \times 4 = 16$$
$$[(2 + 2)^2]^2 = [(4)^2]^2$$
$$= (16)^2 = 256$$
$$(2 \times 2 \times 2)^2 = (8)^2 = 64$$
$$(2 + 2 + 2)^2 = (6)^2 = 36$$

Clearly 256 is the greatest

$\therefore \ [(2 + 2)^2]^2$ is the greatest number.

12. The product of two prime numbers is always composite number.

For example: $2 \times 3 = 6$,
$3 \times 5 = 15$, $5 \times 7 = 35$ etc.

13. 1, 7, 3, 9, 5, 11, ...

Here, two types of series

(*i*) 1, 3, 5, 7, ... and

(*ii*) 7, 9, 11, 13, ...

Hence the next number in the sequence is 7.

14. 87 is not a prime number because it is divided by 3 and 29.

15. Let number $= x$

$$\frac{x}{9} + 9 = 27 \Rightarrow \frac{x}{9} = 27 - 9$$
$$\Rightarrow \quad \frac{x}{9} = 18 \Rightarrow x = 18 \times 9$$
$$= 162$$

Hence number $= 162$.

16. Let the number be x

According to the question,

$$x + 10x = 264$$
$$\Rightarrow \quad 11x = 264$$
$$\Rightarrow \quad x = \frac{264}{11} = 24$$

Hence, number $= 24$

17. Total bananas eaten by Ram
$$= 8 + 5 + 2 = 15$$
$$= \frac{15}{12} \text{ dozen}$$
$$= \frac{5}{4} \text{ dozens} = 1\frac{1}{4} \text{ dozens}.$$

18. Let numbers are x and y
$$x + y = 25 \text{ and } x^2 - y^2 = 75$$
$$\frac{75}{25} = \frac{x^2 - y^2}{x + y} = \frac{(x + y)(x - y)}{(x + y)}$$
$$= x - y$$
$$\Rightarrow 3 = x - y$$

Hence the difference between the numbers $= 3$.

19. John's rank from the last
$$= 51 - 20 = 31.$$

20. $+$ means $\times$

$-$ means $\div$

$\times$ means $+$

$\div$ means $-$

$$(18 + 10 \times 20) - 8 \div 6$$
$$= (18 \times 10 + 20) \div 8 - 6$$
$$= (180 + 20) \div 8 - 6$$
$$= 200 \div 8 - 6 = 25 - 6 = 19.$$

2

SIMPLIFICATION

1. $\sqrt{5^2 + 41 \times 5 - 17^2 - 75} = ?$
   A. 69   B. 61
   C. 71   D. 79

2. $15 - 10 + 5 \times 2 \div 5 = ?$
   A. 70
   B. 4
   C. 5
   D. None of these

3. $10 \times 10 \times 10 \div (20 \div 10 \times 10 - 10) + 6 = ?$
   A. 108   B. 111
   C. 106   D. 114

4. $\dfrac{25}{3} - \dfrac{4}{7}$ of $\dfrac{7}{5} + \dfrac{11}{3} \div \dfrac{2}{3} - 4 = ?$
   A. $8\dfrac{1}{15}$ B. $9\dfrac{1}{30}$
   C. $7\dfrac{1}{30}$ D. $9\dfrac{1}{5}$

5. $\dfrac{9 \div 2 \times 27 \div 9}{18 \div 7.5 \times 5 \div 4} = ?$
   A. 4.5   B. 5.7
   C. 2.5   D. 6.8

6. 37% of 150 − 0.05% of 1000 = ?
   A. 50   B. 55
   C. 55.5   D. 55.55

7. $\dfrac{2.70 \times 2.70 + 4.30 \times 4.30 + 8.60 \times 2.70}{2.70 + 4.30} = ?$

   A. 6.8   B. 7
   C. 7.6   D. 8.5

8. $60 \times [35 - \{25 - (18 - \overline{9-3}) \div 11\}] = ?$
   A. $566\dfrac{5}{7}$ B. $665\dfrac{5}{11}$
   C. $665\dfrac{8}{11}$ D. $765\dfrac{5}{11}$

9. 14% of 255 + ? % of 405 = 124.8
   A. 22   B. 24
   C. 18   D. 15

10. (43% of 2750) − (38% of 2990) = ?
    A. 49.3   B. 44.7
    C. 43.6   D. 46.3

11. $1150 \div 50 \div 23 + 15 = ?$
    A. 16   B. 20
    C. 22   D. 18

12. $\dfrac{140 - 44 \times 9 \div 3}{\dfrac{1}{2} \text{ of } 18 \div 9 + 2} = ?$
    A. $2\dfrac{2}{3}$ B. $3\dfrac{1}{3}$
    C. $4\dfrac{2}{3}$ D. $6\dfrac{4}{5}$

13. $(5967 - 2437 - 1910) \div ? = 27$
    A. 60   B. 50
    C. 65   D. 45

14. $28 \times 104 \div (18 + 6) + 3 = ?$

A. $124\dfrac{1}{3}$ B. $104\dfrac{1}{3}$

C. $125\dfrac{1}{3}$ D. 128

15. $\dfrac{(0.08)^3 + (0.011)^3}{(0.08)^2 - 0.08 \times 0.011 + (0.011)^2} = ?$

A. 0.087 B. 0.091
C. 0.077 D. 0.067

16. $1 + \dfrac{1}{1 + \dfrac{1}{1 + \dfrac{1}{3}}} = ?$

A. $1\dfrac{4}{7}$ B. $2\dfrac{4}{7}$

C. $3\dfrac{4}{7}$ D. $4\dfrac{4}{7}$

17. $\sqrt[3]{12167} \times \sqrt{?} = 621$

A. 841
B. 27
C. 625
D. None of these

18. $0.99 \times 14 \div 11 \div 0.7 = ?$

A. 2.9 B. 1.6
C. 1.8 D. 2.8

19. $22 \div \left[(28 - 13) \div \left\{ (32 - 8) \div \left(5 + \dfrac{1}{3} \right) \right\} \right] = ?$

A. 7.9 B. 6.8
C. 6.6 D. 5.7

20. $3 - \left[9 + \left\{ 14 - (6 - \overline{3 - 21}) \right\} \right] = ?$

A. 0 B. 4
C. 18 D. 6

ANSWERS

1	2	3	4	5	6	7	8	9	10
A	D	C	B	A	B	B	B	A	D

11	12	13	14	15	16	17	18	19	20
A	A	A	A	B	A	D	C	C	B

EXPLANATORY ANSWERS

1. $\sqrt{25 \times 41 \times 5 - 17 \times 17 - 75}$

$= \sqrt{5125 - 289 - 75}$

$= \sqrt{4761} = 69$

2. $15 - 10 + 5 \times 2 \div 5$

$= 15 - 10 + 5 \times \dfrac{2}{5}$

$= 17 - 10 = 7$

3. $10 \times 10 \times 10 \div (20 \div 10 \times 10 - 10) + 6$

$= 10 \times 10 \times 10 \div \left(\dfrac{20}{10} \times 10 - 10 \right) + 6$

$= 10 \times 10 \times 10 \div (20 - 10) + 6$

$= 10 \times 10 \times 10 \div 10 + 6$

$= 10 \times 10 \times 1 + 6$

$= 100 + 6 = 106.$

4. $\dfrac{25}{3} - \dfrac{4}{7}$ of $\dfrac{7}{5} + \dfrac{11}{3} \div \dfrac{2}{3} - 4$

$= \dfrac{25}{3} - \dfrac{4}{5} + \dfrac{11}{3} \div \dfrac{2}{3} - 4$

$= \dfrac{25}{3} - \dfrac{4}{5} + \dfrac{11}{2} - 4 = \dfrac{83}{6} - \dfrac{24}{5}$

$= \dfrac{415 - 144}{30} = \dfrac{271}{30} = 9\dfrac{1}{30}$.

5. $\dfrac{9 \div 2 \times 27 \div 9}{18 \div 7.5 \times 5 \div 4} = \dfrac{\dfrac{9}{2} \times \dfrac{27}{9}}{\dfrac{18}{7.5} \times \dfrac{5}{4}} = \dfrac{\dfrac{27}{2}}{\dfrac{90}{30}}$

$= \dfrac{27}{2} \times \dfrac{30}{90} = \dfrac{9}{2} = 4.5.$

6. 37% of 150 – 0.05% of 1000

$= \dfrac{37}{100}$ of $150 - \dfrac{0.05}{100}$ of 1000

$= \dfrac{111}{2} - \dfrac{5}{10000} \times 1000$

$= 55.5 - .5 = 55.$

7. $\dfrac{\begin{array}{c}2.70 \times 2.70 + 4.30 \times 4.30 \\ + 8.60 \times 2.70\end{array}}{2.70 + 4.30}$

Let $2.70 = a$ and $4.30 = b$

$\dfrac{a^2 + b^2 + 2ab}{a + b} = \dfrac{(a+b)^2}{a+b}$

$= a + b$

$= 2.70 + 4.30 = 7.$

8. $60 \times [35 - \{25 - (18 - \overline{9-3})$
$\div 11\}]$
$= 60 \times [35 - \{25 - (18 - 6) \div 11\}]$
$= 60 \times [35 - \{25 - 12 \div 11\}]$

$= 60 \times \left[35 - \left\{25 - \dfrac{12}{11}\right\}\right]$

$= 60 \times \left[35 - \dfrac{263}{11}\right]$

$= 60 \times \dfrac{122}{11} = 665\dfrac{5}{11}$.

9. 14% of 255 + x% of 405 = 124.8

$\Rightarrow 35.7 + 405 \times \dfrac{x}{100} = 124.8$

$\Rightarrow \dfrac{405 \times x}{100} = 124.8 - 35.7 = 89.1$

$\Rightarrow x = \dfrac{89.1 \times 100}{405} = \dfrac{891 \times 10}{405}$

$= \dfrac{891 \times 2}{81} = 11 \times 2 = 22.$

10. (43% of 2750) – (38% of 2990)
$= 0.43 \times 2750 - 0.38 \times 2990$

$= \dfrac{43}{100} \times 2750 - \dfrac{38}{100} \times 2990$

$= \dfrac{43 \times 275}{10} - \dfrac{38 \times 299}{10}$

$= \dfrac{11825}{10} - \dfrac{11362}{10} = \dfrac{463}{10} = 46.3.$

11. $1150 \div 50 \div 23 + 15$

$= \dfrac{1150}{50} \div 23 + 15$

$= 23 \div 23 + 15 = 1 + 15 = 16.$

12. $\dfrac{140 - 44 \times 9 \div 3}{\dfrac{1}{2} \text{ of } 18 \div 9 + 2} = \dfrac{140 - 44 \times 3}{9 \div 9 + 2}$

$= \dfrac{140 - 132}{1 + 2} = \dfrac{8}{3} = 2\dfrac{2}{3}$.

13. $(5967 - 2437 - 1910) \div x = 27$

$$\frac{1620}{x} = 27 \implies x = \frac{1620}{27} = 60.$$

14. $28 \times 104 \div (18 + 6) + 3$

$= 28 \times 104 \div 24 + 3$

$= 28 \times \dfrac{104}{24} + 3 = 28 \times \dfrac{13}{3} + 3$

$= \dfrac{364}{3} + 3 = \dfrac{373}{3} = 124\dfrac{1}{3}.$

15. $\dfrac{(0.08)^3 + (0.011)^3}{(0.08)^2 - 0.08 \times 0.011 + (0.011)^2}$

Let $0.08 = a$ and $0.011 = b$

$\therefore \dfrac{a^3 + b^3}{a^2 - ab + b^2}$

$= \dfrac{(a+b)(a^2 - ab + b^2)}{(a^2 - ab + b^2)}$

$= a + b = 0.08 + 0.011 = 0.091.$

16. This type of questions is solved starting from the bottom.

$$1 + \cfrac{1}{1 + \cfrac{1}{1 + \cfrac{1}{3}}} = 1 + \cfrac{1}{1 + \cfrac{1}{\cfrac{3+1}{3}}}$$

$$= 1 + \cfrac{1}{1 + \cfrac{3}{4}} = 1 + \cfrac{1}{\cfrac{4+3}{4}}$$

$$= 1 + \dfrac{4}{7} = \dfrac{7+4}{7} = \dfrac{11}{7} = 1\dfrac{4}{7}.$$

17. $\because \ \sqrt[3]{12167} \times \sqrt{x} = 621$

$\Rightarrow 23 \times \sqrt{x} = 621$

$\Rightarrow \sqrt{x} = \dfrac{621}{23} = 27$

$\Rightarrow \left(\sqrt{x}\right)^2 = (27)^2$

$\therefore \ x = 729$

18. $0.99 \times 14 \div 11 \div 0.7$

$= 0.99 \times \dfrac{14}{11} \div 0.7$

$= \dfrac{99}{100} \times \dfrac{14}{11} \times \dfrac{10}{7} = \dfrac{18}{10} = 1.8$

19. $22 \div \left[(28 - 13) \div \left\{ (32 - 8) \div \left(5 + \dfrac{1}{3}\right) \right\} \right]$

$= 22 \div \left[15 \div \left\{ 24 \div \dfrac{16}{3} \right\} \right]$

$= 22 \div \left[15 \div \left\{ 24 \times \dfrac{3}{16} \right\} \right]$

$= 22 \div \left[15 \div \dfrac{9}{2} \right] = 22 \div \left[15 \times \dfrac{2}{9} \right]$

$= 22 \div \dfrac{10}{3} = 22 \times \dfrac{3}{10} = \dfrac{66}{10} = 6.6.$

20. $3 - \left[9 + \left\{ 14 - (6 - \overline{3 - 21}) \right\} \right]$

$= 3 - \left[9 + \left\{ 14 - (6 + 18) \right\} \right]$

$= 3 - [9 + \{14 - 24\}]$

$= 3 - [9 - 10]$

$= 3 + 1 = 4.$

3

CLOCK AND CALENDAR

1. At what time between 5 and 6 are the hands of a clock coincident?
   A. 22 minutes past 5
   B. 30 minutes past 5
   C. $22\frac{8}{11}$ minutes past 5
   D. $27\frac{3}{11}$ minutes past 5

2. On January 12, 1980, it was Saturday. The day of the week on January 12, 1979 was:
   A. Saturday
   B. Friday
   C. Sunday
   D. Thursday

3. At what time between 4 and 5 will the hands of a watch point in opposite directions?
   A. 45 minutes past 4
   B. 40 minutes past 4
   C. $50\frac{4}{11}$ minutes past 4
   D. $54\frac{6}{11}$ minutes past 4

4. Monday falls on 4th April, 1988. What was the day on 3rd November, 1987?
   A. Monday
   B. Sunday
   C. Tuesday
   D. Wednesday

5. At what time between 5.30 and 6 will the hands of a clock be at right angles?

   A. $43\frac{5}{11}$ minutes past 5
   B. $43\frac{7}{11}$ minutes past 5
   C. 40 minutes past 5
   D. 45 minutes past 5

6. How many times do the hands of a clock coincide in a day?
   A. 24
   B. 20
   C. 12
   D. 22

7. What angle do the hands of a clock form at 20 past 7?
   A. 70°
   B. 80°
   C. 90°
   D. 100°

8. What angle is formed when the hour hand is at 6.00 and the minute hand is at 12.00?
   A. 100°
   B. 120°
   C. 180°
   D. 90°

9. What will be the time when the hour hand makes an angle of 50° with the minute hand?
   A. 1.15 hrs
   B. 1.20 hrs
   C. 1.10 hrs
   D. 1.25 hrs

10. There are 5 Saturday in a month. The first day of the month will be:
    A. Sunday
    B. Friday
    C. Wednesday
    D. Monday

11. The first day of the year is Sunday, what day of the week lies

on the first day of the next year?
A. Saturday   B. Friday
C. Monday   D. Thursday

12. The first republic day of India was celebrated on 26th January, 1950. It was:
A. Monday   B. Tuesday
C. Thursday   D. Friday

13. Today is Friday. After 62 days it will be:
A. Friday   B. Thursday
C. Saturday   D. Monday

14. How many days are there from 2nd January 1993 to 15th March 1993?
A. 72   B. 73
C. 74   D. 71

15. If January 1, 1873 was Monday, then the day on January 1, 1874 was?
A. Monday   B. Tuesday
C. Wednesday   D. Thursday

16. What is the time when the hands of the clock make an angle of 90° with each other?
A. 3.10 hrs   B. 3.30 hrs
C. 3.20 hrs   D. 3.25 hrs

17. The angle subtended by the small hand of the clock in 20 minutes will be:
A. 10°   B. 15°
C. 20°   D. 25°

18. How many times the hands of a clock are at right angle in a day?
A. 24   B. 16
C. 44   D. 48

19. The year next to 1988 having the same calendar as that of 1988 is:
A. 1990   B. 1992
C. 1993   D. 1995

20. The year next to 1991 having the same calendar as that of 1990 is:
A. 1998   B. 2001
C. 2002   D. 2003

ANSWERS

1	2	3	4	5	6	7	8	9	10
D	B	D	C	B	D	D	C	A	B

11	12	13	14	15	16	17	18	19	20
C	C	B	B	B	B	A	C	C	C

EXPLANATORY ANSWERS

1. At 5 o'clock, the minute hand is 25 minute spaces apart.

To be coincident, it must gain 25 minutes spaces.

Now, 55 minutes are gained in 60 minutes.

25 minutes will be gained in

$$\left(\frac{60}{55} \times 25\right) \text{ min} = 27\frac{3}{11} \text{ min.}$$

So, the hands are coincident at $27\frac{3}{11}$ minute past 5.

2. The year 1979 being an ordinary year, it has 1 odd day. So, the day on 12th January 1980 is one day beyond the day on 12th January, 1979.

But, January 12, 1980 being Saturday

$\therefore$ January 12, 1979 was Friday.

3. At 4 o'clock, the hands are 20 min. spaces apart. To be in opposite directions, they must be 30 min. spaces apart. So, the minute hand has to gain 50 min. spaces.

Now, 55 min. spaces are gained in 60 min.

50 min. spaces are gained in

$$\left(\frac{60}{55} \times 50\right) \text{ min} = 54\frac{6}{11} \text{ min.}$$

$\therefore$ The hands are in opposite direction at $54\frac{6}{11}$ min. past 4.

4. Counting the number of days from 3rd November, 1987 we have:

Nov. Dec. Jan. Feb. March April
27 + 31 + 31 + 29 + 31 + 4
= 153 days counting 6 odd days.

i.e., (7 – 6) = 1 day beyond the day on 4th April, 1988.

So, the day was Tuesday.

5. At 5 o'clock, the hands are 25 min. spaces apart. To be at right angles and that too between 5.30 and 6, the min. hand has to gain (25 + 15) = 40 min. spaces.

Now 55 min. spaces are gained in 60 min.

$\therefore$ 40 min. spaces are gained in

$$\left(\frac{60}{55} \times 40\right) \text{ min.} = 43\frac{7}{11} \text{ min.}$$

So, the hands are at right angles at $43\frac{7}{11}$ min. past 5.

6. The hands of a clock coincide 11 times in every 12 hrs (because between 11 and 1, they coincide only once, at 12 o'clock).

So, the hands coincide 22 times in a day.

7. The hands of a clock form an angle of 100° at 20 past 7.

8. An angle of 180° is formed when the hour hand is at 6.00 and the minute hand is at 12.00.

9. When the hour hand makes an angle of 50°, the time is 1.15 hrs.

10. In a month of 31 days, three are 4 weeks + 3 days. The three days may be

Thursday, Friday, Saturday
Friday, Saturday, Sunday
Saturday, Monday, Tuesday

The first day of the week may be Thursday, Friday or Saturday.

11. The answer depends on the year. If the year is an ordinary year then next day. If the year is a leap year then beyond 2 days.

Thus, possible answers are Monday or Tuesday.

12. 1949 = 1600 + 300 + 49

Odd day = 0 + 1 + 5 = 6 odd days

Hence 1949 = 6 odd days.

26 days of January contain 5 odd days.

Total odd days = (6 + 5) = 11 or 4 odd days.

So, the day was Thursday

13. Each day of the week is repeated after 7 days.

∴ After 63 days it will be Friday.

So, after 62 days, it would be Thursday.

14.   January = 30 days
February = 28 days
March = 15 days
Total = 73 days

There are 73 days from 2nd January 1993 to 15th March 1993.

15. 1873 is an ordinary year

∴ Number of odd days = 1

This implies the day on December 31, 1873 is Monday.

Hence, required day is Tuesday.

16. The time is 3.30 hrs, when the hands make an angle of 90°.

17. The small hand of the clock rotates 0.5° in one minute. Hence, required angle

$$= 20 \times \frac{5}{10} = 10°$$

18. At 3.00 o'clock and 9.00 o'clock the positions are identical. So, they are at right angle 22 times in 12 hrs.

Thus, in 24 hrs they are 22 × 2 = 44 times at right angles.

19. Starting with 1988, we go on counting the number of odd days till the sum is divisible by 7

Years→ 1988 1989 1990 1991 1992
Odd days 2   1   1   1   2 = 7
                                    i.e., odd days

∴ Calendar for 1993 is the same as that of 1988.

20. We go on counting the odd days from 1991 onwards till the sum is divisible by 7. The number of such days are 14 up to the year 2001.

So, the calendar for 1991 will be repeated in the year 2002.

4

RATIO AND PROPORTION

1. If $x : y : : 5 : 2$, then $8x + 9y : 8x + 2y$ is equal to:
   A. 22 : 29
   B. 29 : 22
   C. 31 : 29
   D. 21 : 29

2. If 76 is divided into the ratios of 7, 5, 3 and 4, then the smallest part will be:
   A. 14
   B. 18
   C. 32
   D. 12

3. The sum of two numbers is 70 and their difference is 16. Ratio of these two numbers is:
   A. 43 : 27
   B. 37 : 64
   C. 43 : 16
   D. 25 : 64

4. Two numbers are in the ratio of 12 and 19. If the sum of these two numbers is 217, the value of smaller number is:
   A. 81
   B. 64
   C. 70
   D. 84

5. If the sum of ₹ 760 is divided by among A, B, C in such a manner that if A gets ₹ 2, B gets ₹ 3 and C gets ₹ 4.5, then the share of C exceeds that of A by:
   A. ₹ 200
   B. ₹ 180
   C. ₹ 215
   D. ₹ 205

6. The ratio of ages of Gulshan and Pankaj is 10 : 9. If Gulshan's age after 6 years be 26 years, then the present age of Pankaj is:
   A. 18 years
   B. 10 years
   C. 17 years
   D. 20 years

7. If a man covers a distance in 7 hrs end a tonga covers the same distance in $4\dfrac{1}{3}$ hrs then what is the ratio of speed of man and tonga?
   A. 7 : 15
   B. 6 : 13
   C. 13 : 21
   D. 13 : 20

8. One year ago the ratio of Tarun and Varun's ages was 4 : 5. If one year after the ratio of their ages is 5 : 6, then find the present age of Tarun.
   A. 7 years
   B. 9 years
   C. 11 years
   D. 6 years

9. What is the value of x if
   $17 : 25 = x : 150$?
   A. 108
   B. 102
   C. 96
   D. 97

10. In what ratio two types of tea costing ₹ 15 per kg and ₹ 20 per kg are mixed so that cost price of the mixture is ₹ 16.50 per kg?
    A. 5 : 6
    B. 7 : 3
    C. 6 : 7
    D. 3 : 7

11. The ratio of ages of Meena and Neetu is 4 : 3. The sum of their

ages is 28 years. After 8 years their ratio of ages will be:

A. 2 : 3   B. 5 : 3

C. 6 : 5   D. 3 : 5

12. Two numbers are in the ratio of 2 : 3. If 8 is added to each of them, they become in the ratio of 3 : 4. The numbers are:

A. 8, 16   B. 16, 24

C. 16, 30   D. 24, 30

13. Two numbers are in the ratio of 3 : 4. If the sum of their squares is 625, find the numbers.

A. 15, 20   B. 10, 15

C. 18, 24   D. 30, 40

14. The number that must be added to each of the numbers 8, 21, 13 and 31 to make the ratio of first two numbers equal to the ratio of last two numbers is:

A. $\dfrac{26}{3}$ B. $\dfrac{11}{3}$

C. 5   D. $\dfrac{16}{3}$

15. If income of A, B and C in the ratio of 9 : 3 : 7 and income of C exceeds the income of B by ₹ 1200 then the income of A is:

A. ₹ 2800   B. ₹ 3100

C. ₹ 2700   D. ₹ 3200

16. The ratio of sides of two squares is 3 : 4. What is the ratio of their perimeters?

A. 3 : 4   B. 2 : 5

C. 4 : 5   D. 3 : 7

17. If $\dfrac{x}{y} = \dfrac{3}{4}$ then what is the value of $(2x + 3y) : (3y - 2x)$?

A. 3 : 1   B. 3 : 2

C. 1 : 2   D. 2 : 3

18. A sum is divided between A, B and C in the ratio 1 : 4 : 7. If difference in shares of A and B is ₹ 2400, then what is the share of C?

A. ₹ 5800   B. ₹ 5600

C. ₹ 7750   D. ₹ 8750

19. The ratio of ages of Om Dutt, Ajay and Sanjay is 9 : 4 : 7. If the difference in ages of Ajay and Sanjay is 9 years, then what is the difference in the ages of Om Dutt and Ajay?

A. 18 years   B. 21 years

C. 15 years   D. 11 years

20. The three angles are in the ratio of 1 : 2 : 3. What is the value of greatest angle?

A. 105°   B. 120°

C. 80°   D. 90°

ANSWERS

1	2	3	4	5	6	7	8	9	10
B	D	A	D	A	A	C	B	B	B

11	12	13	14	15	16	17	18	19	20
C	B	A	C	C	A	A	B	C	D

EXPLANATORY ANSWERS

1. $\because\ x : y :: 5 : 2$

$\Rightarrow\ \dfrac{x}{y} = \dfrac{5}{2}$

$\Rightarrow\ 2x = 5y$ or $8x = 20y$

    [multiply by 4 both sides]

Now $8x + 9y = 20y + 9y$

    [Adding $9y$ both sides]

$\therefore\quad\ 8x + 9y = 29y$

and $\quad 8x + 2y = 20y + 2y = 22y$

Hence, $8x + 9y : 8x + 2y$

$\qquad = 29y : 22y = 29 : 22.$

2. We have to divide 76 in the ratio of $7 : 5 : 3 : 4$

Here, Sum of proportionals

$\qquad = 7 + 5 + 3 + 4 = 19$

$\therefore$ Smallest share $= \dfrac{3}{19} \times 76 = 12.$

3. Let numbers are x and y

$\qquad x + y = 70 \qquad\qquad ...(i)$

and $\ x - y = 16 \qquad\qquad ...(ii)$

Solving (i) and (ii), we get $x = 43$, $y = 27$

$\therefore$ Required ratio $= 43 : 27$

4. Let numbers are $12x$ and $19x$

According to the question,

$\qquad 12x + 19x = 217$

$\Rightarrow\qquad\quad 31x = 217$

$\therefore\qquad\qquad x = \dfrac{217}{31} = 7$

numbers are $12 \times 7 = 84$ and

$\qquad 19 \times 7 = 133$

Hence, the value of smaller number is 84.

5. Ratio of the shares of A, B, and C

$\qquad = 2 : 3 : 4.5 = 20 : 30 : 45$

$\qquad = 4 : 6 : 9$

Sum of proportionals $= 4 + 6 + 9$

$\qquad\qquad\qquad\qquad = 19$

Difference between proportion of C and A

$\qquad = 9 - 4 = 5$

$\therefore$ Share of C exceeds the share of A by

$\qquad \dfrac{5}{19} \times 760 = ₹\ 200.$

6. Let present ages of Gulshan and Pankaj be $10x$ and $9x$.

According to the question,

After 6 years Gulshan's age = 26 years

$\therefore\ 10x + 6 = 26 \ \Rightarrow\ 10x = 20$

$\Rightarrow\qquad\quad x = 2$

Hence, Pankaj's present age

$\qquad = 9 \times 2 = 18$ years.

7. Let distance $= x$ km

Man's speed $= \dfrac{\text{Distance}}{\text{Time}}$

$\qquad\qquad = \dfrac{x}{7}$ km/hr

Tonga's speed $= \dfrac{x}{\dfrac{13}{3}} = \dfrac{3x}{13}$ km/hr

$\therefore$ Required ratio $= \dfrac{x}{7} : \dfrac{3x}{13} = \dfrac{\dfrac{x}{7}}{\dfrac{3x}{13}}$

$\qquad = \dfrac{x}{7} \times \dfrac{13}{3x} = \dfrac{13}{21} = 13 : 21.$

8. Let present ages of Tarun and Varun be x years and y years respectively.

In First case, $\dfrac{x-1}{y-1} = \dfrac{4}{5} \qquad ...(i)$

In Second case, $\dfrac{x+1}{y+1} = \dfrac{5}{6}$ ...(ii)

From (i) and (ii),

$$5x - 4y - 1 = 0 \qquad ...(iii)$$
$$6x - 5y + 1 = 0 \qquad ...(iv)$$

Multiply (iii) by 5 and (iv) by 4, we get,

$$25x - 20y - 5 = 0$$
$$24x - 20y + 4 = 0$$
$$\underline{\quad - \qquad + \qquad - \qquad\qquad}$$
$$x \qquad\qquad - 9 = 0 \Rightarrow x = 9$$

Hence, Tarun's present age = 9 years.

9. $\because \dfrac{17}{25} = \dfrac{x}{150} \Rightarrow 25x = 17 \times 150$

$\Rightarrow x = \dfrac{17 \times 150}{25} = 17 \times 6 = 102$

Hence, the value of $x = 102$.

10. $\because$ Cost of the mixture

$$= ₹ \, 16.50 \text{ per kg}$$

Tea costing ₹ 15 per kg is cheaper from the mixture = ₹ 1.50 per kg

Tea costing ₹ 20 per kg is dearer from the mixture = ₹ 3.50 per kg.

To equal the cost of cheaper and dearer tea, we must multiply them by 3.50 and 1.50 respectively, i.e., in the ratio of 7 : 3

Hence Required ratio

$$= \dfrac{3.50}{1.50} = \dfrac{35}{15} = 7 : 3$$

11. Let present ages of Meena and Neetu be $4x$ years and $3x$ years respectively.

$4x + 3x = 28 \Rightarrow 7x = 28 \Rightarrow x = 4$

$\therefore$ Meena's age = $4 \times 4 = 16$ years

Neetu's age = $3 \times 4 = 12$ years.

After 8 years, Meena's age

$$= 16 + 8 = 24 \text{ years}$$

After 8 years, Neetu's age

$$= 12 + 8 = 20 \text{ years}$$

Required ratio = $\dfrac{24}{20} = \dfrac{6}{5} = 6 : 5$.

12. Let numbers are $2x$ and $3x$ respectively.

According to the question,

$$\dfrac{2x+8}{3x+8} = \dfrac{3}{4}$$
$$\Rightarrow \quad 9x + 24 = 8x + 32$$
$$\Rightarrow \qquad\qquad x = 32 - 24 = 8$$
$$2x = 2 \times 8 = 16$$
$$3x = 3 \times 8 = 24$$

Hence, numbers are 16 and 24.

13. Let numbers are $3x$ and $4x$ respectively.

According to the question,

$$(3x)^2 + (4x)^2 = 625$$
$$\Rightarrow \quad 9x^2 + 16x^2 = 625$$
$$\Rightarrow \qquad\quad 25x^2 = 625$$
$$\Rightarrow \qquad\quad x^2 = \dfrac{625}{25} = 25$$
$$\Rightarrow \qquad\quad x = 5$$

Hence, numbers are 15 and 20

$$\begin{bmatrix} \because \; 3x = 3 \times 5 = 15 \\ 4x = 4 \times 5 = 20 \end{bmatrix}$$

14. Let x be added to each of them

According to the question,

$$\dfrac{x+8}{21+x} = \dfrac{x+13}{31+x}$$
$$\Rightarrow (x + 8)(31 + x) = (x + 13)(21 + x)$$
$$\Rightarrow 31x + x^2 + 248 + 8x = 21x + x^2 + 273 + 13x$$
$$\Rightarrow 39x - 34x = 273 - 248$$
$$\Rightarrow \qquad 5x = 25 \Rightarrow x = 5$$

Hence, 5 should be added to each of the given numbers.

15. Let income of A, B, C are $9x$, $3x$ and $7x$ respectively

According to the question,

$$7x - 3x = 1200 \Rightarrow 4x = 1200$$
$$\Rightarrow \qquad x = 300$$

Hence, income of A $= 9x$
$$= 9 \times 300 = ₹\ 2700$$

16. Let sides of the squares be $3x$ and $4x$ respectively.

Perimeter of first square
$$= 4 \times 3x = 12x$$

Perimeter of 2nd square
$$= 4x \times 4 = 16x$$

Required ratio $= \dfrac{12x}{16x} = \dfrac{3}{4} = 3 : 4.$

17. $\dfrac{x}{y} = \dfrac{3}{4} \quad \Rightarrow \quad 4x = 3y$

Now, $2x + 3y = 2x + 4x = 6x$

and $3y - 2x = 4x - 2x = 2x$
$$[\because 4x = 3y]$$

$\therefore (2x + 3y) : (3y - 2x) = 6x : 2x$
$$= 3 : 1.$$

18. Difference in ratio of A and B
$$= 4 - 1 = 3$$

$\therefore$ Share of C $= \dfrac{7}{3} \times 2400$
$$= ₹\ 5600.$$

19. Let the ages of Om Dutt, Ajay and Sanjay are $9x$, $4x$ and $7x$ respectively.

According to the question,
$$7x - 4x = 9$$
$$\Rightarrow \qquad 3x = 9 \Rightarrow x = 3$$

$\therefore$ Age of Om Dutt $= 9 \times 3$
$$= 27 \text{ years}$$

Age of Ajay $= 4 \times 3 = 12$ years

Difference in their ages
$$= 27 - 12 = 15 \text{ years}$$

20. $x + 2x + 3x = 180°$
$$\Rightarrow \qquad 6x = 180°$$
$$\Rightarrow \qquad x = 30°$$

Hence, the value of greatest angle
$$= 3 \times 30 = 90°$$

5

PARTNERSHIP

1. Three partners A, B and C invest ₹ 13000, ₹ 17000 and ₹ 5000 respectively in a business. They have a profit of ₹ 1750. B's share of profit is:
   A. ₹ 650
   B. ₹ 850
   C. ₹ 350
   D. ₹ 550

2. A and B enter into partnership investing ₹ 12000 and ₹ 16000 respectively. After 8 months, C, also joins the business with a capital of ₹ 15000. The share of C in a profit of ₹ 45600 after 2 years will be:
   A. ₹ 12000
   B. ₹ 13200
   C. ₹ 17400
   D. ₹ 18000

3. A starts a business with ₹ 30000 and 4 months later B joins. If at the end of the year, the profits are divided by A and B in the proportion of 9 : 4, B's capital was:
   A. ₹ 18000
   B. ₹ 22000
   C. ₹ 20000
   D. ₹ 19000

4. A, B and C invest ₹ 2000, ₹ 3000 and ₹ 4000 in a business. After one year A removed his money. B and C continued the business for one more year. If the net profit after 2 years be ₹ 3200, the A's share in the profit is:
   A. ₹ 700
   B. ₹ 900
   C. ₹ 500
   D. ₹ 400

5. Dilip, Ram and Amar started a shop by investing ₹ 2700, ₹ 8100 and ₹ 7200 respectively. At the and of one year, the profit was distributed. If Ram's share was ₹ 3600, their total profit was:
   A. ₹ 9000
   B. ₹ 12000
   C. ₹ 8000
   D. ₹ 6000

6. Suresh invested ₹ 12000 in a business and Dinesh joined him after 4 months by investing ₹ 7000. If the net profit after one year be ₹ 13300, Dinesh's share in the profit is:
   A. ₹ 3724
   B. ₹ 4248
   C. ₹ 3612
   D. ₹ 3840

7. A, B and C contract a work for ₹ 550. Together A and B are to do $\frac{7}{11}$ of the work. The share of C should be:
   A. ₹ 400
   B. ₹ 300
   C. ₹ 200
   D. ₹ $183\frac{1}{3}$

8. A and B started a business with the investment of ₹ 80000 and ₹ 60000 respectively. At the end of the year total profit in the business will be divided between them in the ratio of:
   A. 2 : 3
   B. 3 : 4
   C. 2 : 1
   D. 4 : 3

9. A and B started a business in partnership with the investment of ₹ 4000 and ₹ 6000 respectively. If at the end of the year total profit is ₹ 2250, what will each of them get?
A. ₹ 900, ₹ 1350
B. ₹ 800, ₹ 1450
C. ₹ 1000, ₹ 1250
D. ₹ 1200, ₹ 1050

10. Sonu, Monu and Mohit together start a business with the investment of ₹ 1800, ₹ 1500 and ₹ 1600 respectively. If at the end of the year, Monu gains a profit of ₹ 900, the total profit in the business is:
A. ₹ 2880   B. ₹ 2940
C. ₹ 3200   D. ₹ 3240

11. Om Dutt started a business with a capital of ₹ 8000. After six months, Sanjay joined him with investment of some capital. If at the end of the year each of them gets equal amount as profit, how much did Sanjay invest in the business?
A. ₹ 18000   B. ₹ 17500
C. ₹ 16000   D. ₹ 16500

12. A, B and C buy a farm for ₹ 100000. A contributes ₹ 40000 in it. They sell it, and from the profit B gets ₹ 2750 and C gets ₹ 1750. What would be the profit of A?
A. ₹ 2780   B. ₹ 3000
C. ₹ 3280   D. ₹ 2785

13. A and B jointly invest ₹ 2100 and ₹ 3100 respectively in a firm. A is in active partner and hence he gets 25% of the profit separately. If their business yields them total ₹ 1040 as profit, what will be the gain of each of them?
A. ₹ 415, ₹ 625
B. ₹ 575, ₹ 465
C. ₹ 515, ₹ 525
D. ₹ 560, ₹ 480

14. Two partners invested ₹ 12500 and ₹ 8500 respectively in a business and decided that 60% of the profit incurred from the business will be equally divided between them while remaining profit will be assumed as interest on their capitals. If one of the partners gets ₹ 300 more profit than the other, what is the total profit in the business?
A. ₹ 3937.50   B. ₹ 4940.50
C. ₹ 3936.50   D. ₹ 4156

15. Neeraj and Birju are partner in a business. They divide between them the profit incurred in the business in such a proportion that $\frac{2}{5}$ th portion of the profit gained by Neeraj is equal to $\frac{1}{3}$ rd portion of the profit gained by Birju. If total profit in the business is ₹ 1210, find the profit earned by Birju.
A. ₹ 780   B. ₹ 550
C. ₹ 680   D. ₹ 590

16. A, B and C start a business, A invests 3 times as much as B invests and B invests two-third of what C invests. Then, the ratio of capitals of A, B and C is:

A. 3 : 9 : 2   B. 6 : 10 : 15
C. 5 : 3 : 2   D. 6 : 2 : 3

17. Rama and Pooja are partners in a business. Rama invests ₹ 5000 for 5 months and Pooja invests ₹ 6000 for 6 months. If the total profit is ₹ 610, then Pooja's share in the profit is:
A. ₹ 250   B. ₹ 360
C. ₹ 520   D. ₹ 630

18. Ashok invests ₹ 3000 for a year and Sunil joins him with ₹ 2000 after 4 months. After the they receive a return of ₹ 2600. Sunil's share is:
A. ₹ 800   B. ₹ 1000
C. ₹ 750   D. ₹ 900

19. Kishan and Nandan started a joint firm. Kishan's investment was thrice the investment of Nandan and the period of his investment was two times the period of investment of Nandan. Nandan got ₹ 4000 as profit for his investment. Their total profit if the distribution of profit is directly proportional to the period and amount is:
A. ₹ 24000   B. ₹ 16000
C. ₹ 28000   D. ₹ 20000

20. A, B and C enter into partnership by making investments in the ratio 3 : 5 : 7. After a year, C invests another ₹ 337600 while A withdraws ₹ 45600. The ratio of investments then changes to 24 : 59 : 167. How much did A invest initially?
A. ₹ 45600
B. ₹ 96000
C. ₹ 141600
D. None of these

ANSWERS

1	2	3	4	5	6	7	8	9	10
B	A	C	D	C	A	C	D	A	B

11	12	13	14	15	16	17	18	19	20
C	B	B	A	B	D	A	A	C	C

EXPLANATORY ANSWERS

1. Ratio of investments of A, B, C
= 13000 : 17000 : 5000
= 13 : 17 : 5

∴ B's share = $₹\left(1750 \times \dfrac{17}{35}\right)$

= ₹ 850.

2. Ratio of capitals of A, B, C
= (12000 × 24) : (16000 × 24) : (15000 × 16)

= 6 : 8 : 5

C's share = $₹\left(45600 \times \dfrac{5}{19}\right)$

= ₹ 12000.

3. Let B's capital be ₹ x. Then,

$$\frac{30000 \times 12}{x \times 8} = \frac{9}{4}$$

⇒ x = ₹ 20000.

4. Ratio of investments
$$= (2000 \times 1) : (3000 \times 2) : (4000 \times 2)$$
$$= 1 : 3 : 4$$

$$\therefore \text{ A's share } = ₹\left(3200 \times \frac{1}{8}\right)$$
$$= ₹ 400.$$

5. Ratio of shares of Dilip, Ram and Amar
$$= 2700 : 8100 : 7200 = 3 : 9 : 8$$
If Ram's share is ₹ 9, total profit
$$= ₹ 20$$
If Ram's share is ₹ 3600, total profit $= \dfrac{20}{9} \times 3600 = ₹ 8000.$

6. Ratio of investments
$$= (12000 \times 12) : (7000 \times 8)$$
$$= 18 : 7$$
Dinesh's share in the profit
$$= 13300 \times \frac{7}{25} = ₹ 3724$$

7. C's share $= ₹\left(550 \times \dfrac{4}{11}\right) = ₹ 200.$

8. The two partners invest their capitals for the same period.

$\therefore$ Profit will be divided between them in the ratio of their capitals.

$\therefore$ Ratio between their profits
$$= 80000 : 60000 = 4 : 3.$$

9. It is clear that A and B invest their capitals for the same period.

Ratio between the profits of A and B
$$= 4000 : 6000 = 2 : 3$$
Sum of proportionals $= 2 + 3 = 5$

A's share in the profit $= \dfrac{2}{5} \times 2250$
$$= ₹ 900$$

B's share in the profit $= \dfrac{3}{5} \times 2250$
$$= ₹ 1350.$$

10. Sonu, Monu and Mohit invest their capitals for the same period.

$\therefore$ Ratio of their profits
$$= 1800 : 1500 : 1600$$
$$= 18 : 15 : 16$$
Sum of proportionals
$$= 18 + 15 + 16 = 49$$
Monu's profit $= ₹ 900$

$\therefore$ Total profit in the business
$$= \frac{900}{15} \times 49 = ₹ 2940.$$

11. Investment by Om Dutt $= ₹ 8000$ for 12 months.

$\therefore$ Capital of Om Dutt
$$= ₹ 8000 \times 12$$
$$= ₹ 96000 \text{ for 1 month}$$
Let Sanjay invested ₹ x for 6 months

$\therefore$ Capital of Sanjay $= ₹ 6 \times x$
$$= ₹ 6x \text{ for 1 month}$$
Since they get equal amounts as profit

$\therefore$ Their investment will also be same

Therefore, $6x = 96000$
$$\Rightarrow \quad x = \frac{96000}{6}$$
$$= ₹ 16000.$$

12. Capital of $(A + B + C) = ₹ 100000$
Capital of A $= ₹ 40000$
$\therefore$ Capital of $(B + C)$
$$= 100000 - 40000 = ₹ 60000$$
Profit of $(B + C) = (2750 + 1750)$
$$= ₹ 4500$$

$\therefore$ A's profit $= 4500 \times \dfrac{40000}{60000}$
$$= ₹ 3000.$$

13. Total profit in the business
$$= ₹\ 1040$$
Separate profit for A = 25% of ₹1040
$$= \frac{1040 \times 25}{100} = ₹\ 260$$
Remaining profit = (1040 − 260)
$$= ₹\ 780$$
The remaining profit will be divided in the proportion of their capitals

∴ Ratio between capitals of A and B = 2100 : 3100 = 21 : 31

Sum of proportionals = 21 + 31
$$= 52$$
∴ A's profit $= \dfrac{21}{52} \times 780 = ₹\ 315$

B's profit $= \dfrac{31}{52} \times 780 = ₹\ 465$

Total profit of A = (315 + 260)
$$= ₹\ 575$$

14. Let total profit in the business
$$= ₹\ x$$
∴ 60% of total profit
$$= 60\% \text{ of } x = ₹\frac{3x}{5}$$
The two partners will get profit of $₹\dfrac{3x}{10}$ and $₹\dfrac{3x}{10}$ respectively

∴ Remaining profit $= x - \dfrac{3x}{5}$
$$= ₹\frac{2x}{5}$$
The remaining profit assumed as interest on the capital will be divided in the proportion of their capital's.

Ratio between their capitals
$$= 12500 : 8500 = 25 : 17$$
Sum of proportionals
$$= 25 + 17 = 42$$
1st partner's profit $= \dfrac{25}{42} \times \dfrac{2x}{5}$
$$= ₹\frac{5x}{21}$$
2nd partner's profit $= \dfrac{17}{42} \times \dfrac{2x}{5}$
$$= ₹\frac{17x}{105}$$
According to the question,
$$\frac{3x}{10} + \frac{5x}{21} = \frac{3x}{10} + \frac{17x}{105} + 300$$
$$\therefore \quad \frac{8x}{105} = 300 \Rightarrow x = \frac{105 \times 300}{8}$$
$$= ₹\ 3937.50$$
∴ Total profit in the business
$$= ₹\ 3937.50$$

15. According to the question, 2/5th portion of profit made by Neeraj
$$= \frac{1}{3}\text{rd portion of profit made by Birju}$$
∴ Ratio between profits of Neeraj and Birju
$$= \frac{2}{5} : \frac{1}{3} = 6 : 5$$
where total profit = ₹ 1210

In the above proportion, sum of proportionals
$$= 6 + 5 = 11$$
∴ Share of Birju in the profit
$$= \frac{5}{11} \times 1210 = ₹\ 550.$$

16. Suppose C invests ₹ x, then

B invests ₹ $\dfrac{2x}{3}$ and A invests ₹ $2x$

Ratio of investments of A, B, C

$$= 2x : \dfrac{2x}{3} : x$$
$$= 6 : 2 : 3.$$

17. Ratio of capitals
$$= (5000 \times 5) : (6000 \times 6)$$
$$= 25000 : 36000$$
$$= 25 : 36$$

Pooja's share $= \dfrac{25}{61} \times 610 = ₹\,250.$

18. Ratio of capitals
$$= 3000 \times 12 : 2000 \times 8$$
$$= 36000 : 16000 = 9 : 4$$

∴ Sunil's share $= \dfrac{4}{13} \times 2600$
$$= ₹\ 800.$$

19. Let Nandan's investment be ₹ x for y months

Then, Kishan's investment is ₹ $3x$ for $2y$ months

∴ Ratio of their investments
$$= xy : 6xy = 1 : 6$$

Nandan's share = ₹ 4000

Kishan's share = ₹ 24000

∴ Total profit = ₹ 28000.

20. Let the initial investments of A, B, C be ₹ $3x$, ₹ $5x$ and ₹ $7x$ respectively. Then,
$$(3x - 45600) : 5x : (7x + 337600)$$
$$= 24 : 59 : 167$$

∴ $\dfrac{3x - 45600}{5x} = \dfrac{24}{59}$

⇒ $x = 47200$

∴ A invested initially
$$= ₹(47200 \times 3) = ₹\ 141600.$$

6
AVERAGE

1. The average of first-five multiple of 3 :
   A. 6
   B. 9
   C. 3
   D. 12

2. The average of 50 number, is 38. If two numbers namely, 45 and 55 are discarted, the average of remaining number is:
   A. 36.50
   B. 37.00
   C. 37.50
   D. 37.52

3. The average age of an adult class is 40 years. 12 new students with an average age of 32 years join the class, there by decreasing the average of the class by 4 years. The original strength of the class was:
   A. 10
   B. 11
   C. 12
   D. 15

4. The average temperature of first three-days is 27°C and of the next 3 days is 29°C. If the average of the whole week is 28.5°C, the temperature of the last day is:
   A. 31.5°C
   B. 10.5°C
   C. 21°C
   D. 42°C

5. The average weight of 3 men, A, B and C is 84 kg. Another man D joins the group and the average now becomes 80 kg. If another man E, whose weight is 3 kg more than that of D, replace A, then average weight of B, C, D and E becomes 79 kg. The weight of A is:
   A. 70 kg
   B. 72 kg
   C. 75 kg
   D. 80 kg

6. The average of 30 results is 20 and the average of other 20 results is 30. The average of all the results is:
   A. 25
   B. 24
   C. 50
   D. 48

7. The average height of 30 girls out of a class of 40 is 160 cms and that of the remaining girls is 156 cms. The average height of the whole class is:
   A. 158 cm
   B. 158.5 cm
   C. 159 cm
   D. 159.5 cm

8. A Ship sails out to a mark at the rate of 15 km/hr and sails back at the rate of 10 km/hr. The average rate of sailing is:
   A. 12.5 km/hr
   B. 12 km/hr
   C. 25 km/hr
   D. 5 km/hr

9. A cricketer scored 180 runs in the first test and 258 runs in the second. How many runs should he score in the third test so that his average score in the three tests would be 230 runs?

A. 219
B. 242
C. 334
D. None of these

10. The average age of A, B, C, D 5 years ago was 45 years. By including X, the present average of all five is 49 years the present age of X is:
A. 64 years   B. 48 years
C. 45 years   D. 40 years

11. The average age of three boys is 15 years. If their ages are in ratio 3 : 5 : 7, the age of the youngest boy is:
A. 21 years   B. 18 years
C. 15 years   D. 9 years

12. The sum of three numbers is 98. If the ratio between first and second be 2 : 3 and that of between second and third be 5 : 8, then second number is:
A. 30   B. 20
C. 58   D. 48

13. The average weight of A, B, C is 45 kg. If the average weight of A and B be 40 kg and that of B and C be 43 kg, then the weight of B is:
A. 17 kg   B. 20 kg
C. 26 kg   D. 31 kg

14. The average salary of 20 workers in an office is ₹ 1900 per month. If the manager's salary is added, the average becomes ₹ 2000 per month. The manager's salary is:
A. ₹ 24000
B. ₹ 25200
C. ₹ 45600
D. None of these

15. The average of first-five prime numbers is:
A. 5.0   B. 5.2
C. 5.6   D. 6.0

16. The average of 25 results is 18; that of first 12 is 14 and of the last 12 is 17. Thirteenth result is:
A. 78   B. 85
C. 28   D. 72

17. The average age of a committee of seven trustees is the same as it was 5 years ago; a young man having been substituted for one of them. The new man compared to the replaced old man, is younger in age by:
A. 5 years   B. 7 years
C. 12 years   D. 35 years

18. The average expenditure of a man for the first five months is ₹ 120 and for the next seven months is ₹ 130. His monthly average income if he saves ₹ 290 in that year, is:
A. ₹ 160   B. ₹ 170
C. ₹ 150   D. ₹ 140

19. The mean of 50 observations was 36. It was found latter that an observation 48 was wrongly taken as 23. The correct new mean is:
A. 39.1   B. 36.5
C. 36.1   D. 35.2

20. Out of three numbers, the first is twice the second and is half of the third. If the average of the three numbers is 56, the three numbers in order are:
A. 48, 96, 24   B. 48, 24, 96
C. 96, 24, 48   D. 96, 48, 24

ANSWERS

1	2	3	4	5	6	7	8	9	10
B	C	C	A	C	B	C	B	D	C

11	12	13	14	15	16	17	18	19	20
D	A	D	D	C	A	D	C	B	B

EXPLANATORY ANSWERS

1. First five multiple of 3 are

3, 6, 9, 12 and 15

$$\text{Average} = \frac{3+6+9+12+15}{5}$$

$$= \frac{45}{5} = 9.$$

2. Total of 50 numbers $= 50 \times 38$

$$= 1900$$

Average of 48 numbers

$$= \frac{1900-(55+45)}{48} = \frac{1800}{48}$$

$$= \frac{75}{2} = 37.50.$$

3. Let the original strength of the class $= x$

According to the question,

$$40x + 12 \times 32 = (x + 12) \times 36$$
$$\Rightarrow 40x + 12 \times 32 = 36x + 12 \times 36$$
$$\Rightarrow 40x - 36x = 12 \times 36 - 12 \times 32$$
$$\Rightarrow 4x = 12 (36 - 32)$$
$$\Rightarrow 4x = 12 \times 4$$
$$\Rightarrow x = \frac{12 \times 4}{4} = 12$$

Hence, the original strength of the class $= 12$.

4. Total temp. of first 3 days

$$= 27 \times 3 = 81°C$$

Total temp. of next 3 days

$$= 29 \times 3 = 87°C$$

Total temp. of the week

$$= 28.5 \times 7 = 199.5°C$$

$\therefore$ Temp. of the last day

$$= 199.5°C - (81 + 87)°C$$
$$= 199.5 - 168 = 31.5°C.$$

5. Weight of (A + B + C)

$$= 84 \times 3 = 252 \text{ kg}$$

Weight of D $= (80 \times 4 - 84 \times 3)$

$$= 320 - 252 = 68 \text{ kg}$$

Weight of E $= (68 + 3) = 71$ kg

(B + C + D + E)'s weight

$$= 79 \times 4 = 316 \text{ kg}$$

(A + B + C + D + E)'s weight

$$= 252 + 68 + 71 = 391 \text{ kg}$$

$\therefore$ Weight of A $= 391 - 316$

$$= 75 \text{ kg.}$$

6. Total of 30 results $= 30 \times 20$

$$= 600$$

Total of 20 results $= 20 \times 30$

$$= 600$$

Total of 50 results $= 600 + 600$

$$= 1200$$

Average of 50 result $= \dfrac{1200}{50} = 24.$

7. Total height of 30 girls

$$= 30 \times 160 = 4800 \text{ cm}$$

Total height of remaining 10 girls

$$= 10 \times 156 = 1560 \text{ cm}$$

Total height of 40 girls

$$= 4800 + 1560 = 6360 \text{ cm}$$

$$\text{Average of 40 girls} = \frac{6360}{40}$$
$$= 159 \text{ cm.}$$

8. Average speed $= \left(\dfrac{2xy}{x+y}\right)$ km/hr

$$= \left(\frac{2 \times 15 \times 10}{(15+10)}\right) \text{ km/hr}$$

$$= \left(\frac{2 \times 15 \times 10}{25}\right) \text{ km/hr}$$

$$= 12 \text{ km/hr.}$$

9. Let the runs he should score in third test be x. Then,

$$\frac{180+258+x}{3} = 230$$
$$\Rightarrow\ 438 + x = 690$$
$$\Rightarrow\qquad x = 690 - 438 = 252.$$

10. Total age of A, B, C, D 5 years ago

$$= (45 \times 4) = 180 \text{ years}$$

Total present age of A, B, C, D and X

$$= (49 \times 5) = 245 \text{ years}$$

Present age of A, B, C, D

$$= 180 + 20 = 200 \text{ years}$$

$\therefore$ Present age of X $= 245 - 200$
$$= 45 \text{ years.}$$

11. Total age of 3 boys $= 15 \times 3$
$$= 45 \text{ years}$$
$$3x + 5x + 7x = 45$$
$$\Rightarrow 15x = 45 \ \Rightarrow\ x = 3$$

Age of the youngest boy
$$= 3 \times 3 = 9 \text{ years.}$$

12. Let the numbers are x, y and z

$$\frac{x}{y} = \frac{2}{3} \text{ and } \frac{y}{z} = \frac{5}{8}$$

$$\Rightarrow x = \frac{2y}{3} \text{ and } z = \frac{8y}{5}$$

$$\because\qquad x + y + z = 98$$

$$\Rightarrow\quad \frac{2y}{3} + y + \frac{8y}{5} = 98$$

$$\Rightarrow \frac{10y + 15y + 24y}{15} = 98$$

$$\Rightarrow\qquad 49y = 15 \times 98$$

$$\Rightarrow\qquad y = \frac{15 \times 98}{49}$$

$$= 15 \times 2 = 30$$

Hence, 2nd number $= 30$.

13. Total weight of (A + B + C)
$$= 45 \times 3 = 135 \text{ kg}$$
Total weight of (A + B)
$$= 40 \times 2 = 80 \text{ kg}$$
Weight of C $= 135 - 80 = 55$ kg
Total weight of (B + C)
$$= 43 \times 2 = 36 \text{ kg}$$
Weight of B $= 86 - 85 = 31$ kg.

14. Total monthly salary of 20 workers
$$= 20 \times 1900 = ₹\ 38000$$
Total monthly salary with manager
$$= 21 \times 2000 = ₹\ 42000$$
Monthly salary of manager
$$= ₹\ 4000$$
Annual salary of manager
$$= ₹\ 48000.$$

15. First five prime numbers are
2, 3, 5, 7 and 11

$$\text{Average} = \frac{2+3+5+7+11}{5}$$

$$= \frac{28}{5} = 5.6.$$

16. Thirteenth result
$$= 25 \times 18 - (14 \times 12 + 17 \times 12)$$
$$= 450 - (168 + 204)$$
$$= 450 - 372 = 78.$$

17. During these 5 years, the total age would have increased by (7×5) = 35 years

But, it remains the same as it was 5 years ago.

$\therefore$ The new man is younger than the replaced old man by 35 years.

18. Total income for 12 months
$= (120 \times 5 + 130 \times 7 + 290)$
$= ₹ 1800$

$\therefore$ Average monthly income

$$= \frac{1800}{12} = ₹ 150.$$

19. Total of 50 observations
$= 50 \times 36 = 1800$

Increased number $= 48 - 23 = 25$
New total number $= 1800 + 25$
$\qquad\qquad\qquad\quad = 1825$

$$\text{Correct mean} = \frac{1825}{50} = 36.5.$$

20. Let the numbers be $2x$, x and $4x$.

$$\text{Average} = \frac{2x + x + 4x}{3} = \frac{7x}{3}$$

According to the question,

$$\frac{7x}{3} = 56$$

$$\Rightarrow \quad x = 24$$

Hence, the numbers in order are 48, 24 and 96.

7

SIMPLE AND COMPOUND INTEREST

1. The simple interest on ₹ 500 for 6 years at 5% p.a. is:
   - A. ₹ 250
   - B. ₹ 150
   - C. ₹ 140
   - D. ₹ 120

2. If the simple interest on a certain sum of money at 6% per annum for 3 years is ₹ 90, the sum will be:
   - A. ₹ 500
   - B. ₹ 450
   - C. ₹ 525
   - D. ₹ 560

3. A sum of money doubles itself in 20 years. In how many years will it treble itself at the same rate of simple interest?
   - A. 30 years
   - B. 50 years
   - C. 40 years
   - D. 45 years

4. If the simple interest on ₹ 500 for 4 years is ₹ 40, the rate of interest is:
   - A. $3\frac{1}{2}\%$
   - B. 2%
   - C. $2\frac{1}{2}\%$
   - D. 3%

5. A man will get ₹ 87 as simple interest on ₹ 725 at 4% per annum in:
   - A. 3 years
   - B. $3\frac{1}{2}$ years
   - C. 4 years
   - D. 5 years

6. A invested ₹ 5000 at a certain rate of simple interest and ₹ 4000 at 1% higher rate of interest. If the interest in both cases is same, the former rate of interest is:
   - A. 3%
   - B. 4%
   - C. 6%
   - D. 5%

7. A man lends ₹ 500 for 4 years and ₹ 600 for 3 years at a certain rate of simple interest. If he gets total ₹ 190 as interest in both cases, the rate percent per annum is:
   - A. 8%
   - B. 5%
   - C. 10%
   - D. 4%

8. Which of the following sum of money will amount to ₹ 1050 in 5 years at 8% per annum simple interest?
   - A. ₹ 750
   - B. ₹ 825
   - C. ₹ 775
   - D. ₹ 730

9. A certain sum of money lent out on simple interest amount to ₹ 1760 in 2 years and to ₹ 2000 in 5 years. Find the sum:
   - A. ₹ 1650
   - B. ₹ 1500
   - C. ₹ 1580
   - D. ₹ 1600

10. After what time will the sum of ₹ 2000 become ₹ 2240 at 4% per annum simple interest?

A. 3 years B. 2 years
C. 5 years D. 4 years

11. What will be the compound interest on ₹ 8000 for 3 years at 5% p.a.?
A. ₹ 1361 B. ₹ 1261
C. ₹ 1260 D. ₹ 1250

12. Find the amount of ₹ 4000 borrowed for 2 years at $2\dfrac{1}{2}$ % per annum compound interest.
A. ₹ 4202.50 B. ₹ 4102.50
C. ₹ 5202.50 D. ₹ 4000.50

13. After how many years will ₹ 3375 become ₹ 4096 at $6\dfrac{2}{3}$% per annum compound interest?
A. 4 years B. 2 years
C. $2\dfrac{1}{2}$ years D. 3 years

14. A certain sum of money placed at compound interest amounts to ₹ 110 in 1 year and ₹ 121 in 2 years. The rate of interest per annum is:
A. 5% B. 10%
C. 8% D. 4%

15. The difference between compound and simple interest on a certain sum of money for 2 years at 5% per annum is ₹ 21. Find the sum.
A. ₹ 7200 B. ₹ 8400
C. ₹ 9200 D. ₹ 8500

16. The difference between simple interest and the compound interest on a certain sum of money for 2 years at 10% is ₹ 8. The sum is:
A. ₹ 1600 B. ₹ 800
C. ₹ 1200 D. ₹ 640

17. ₹ 800 at 5% per annum compound interest amount to ₹ 882 in:
A. 4 years B. 3 years
C. 2 years D. 1 year

18. A sum amounts to ₹ 1352 in 2 years at 4% compound interest. The sum is:
A. ₹ 1300 B. ₹ 1200
C. ₹ 1250 D. ₹ 1260

19. At what rate percent compound interest will ₹ 625 amount to ₹ 900 in 2 years?
A. 20% B. 15%
C. 30% D. 25%

20. The compound interest on a certain sum of money for 2 years at 10% per annum is ₹ 420. The simple interest on the same sum at the same rate and same time will be:
A. ₹ 350 B. ₹ 375
C. ₹ 380 D. ₹ 400

ANSWERS

1	2	3	4	5	6	7	8	9	10
B	A	C	B	A	B	B	A	D	A

11	12	13	14	15	16	17	18	19	20
B	A	D	B	B	B	C	C	A	D

EXPLANATORY ANSWERS

1. $\text{S.I.} = \dfrac{p \times r \times t}{100} = \dfrac{500 \times 5 \times 6}{100}$

$$= ₹\ 150.$$

2. $P = \dfrac{\text{SI} \times 100}{r \times t} = \dfrac{90 \times 100}{6 \times 3} = ₹\ 500.$

3. In the first case,

$$P = ₹\ x,\ \ A = ₹\ 2x$$
$$t = 20 \text{ years}$$
$$\text{SI} = A - P = 2x - x = ₹\ x$$

$$r = \dfrac{\text{SI} \times 100}{p \times t} = \dfrac{x \times 100}{x \times 20}$$

$$= 5\%$$

In the second case,

$$P = ₹\ x,\ \ A = ₹\ 3x$$
$$\text{rate} = 5\%$$
$$\text{SI} = A - P = 3x - x = 2x$$

$$\therefore \quad t = \dfrac{\text{SI} \times 100}{p \times r} = \dfrac{2x \times 100}{x \times 5}$$

$$= 40 \text{ years}$$

Therefore, the sum will treble itself in 40 years.

4. $\text{Rate} = \dfrac{\text{SI} \times 100}{p \times t} = \dfrac{40 \times 100}{500 \times 4} = 2\%.$

5. $\text{Time} = \dfrac{\text{SI} \times 100}{p \times r} = \dfrac{87 \times 100}{725 \times 4}$

$$= 3 \text{ years.}$$

6. In the first case,

$$\text{SI} = \dfrac{5000 \times x \times t}{100}$$

In the 2nd case,

$$\text{SI} = \dfrac{4000 \times (x+1) \times t}{100}$$

According to the question,

$$\dfrac{5000 \times x \times t}{100} = \dfrac{4000 \times (x+1) \times t}{100}$$

$$\Rightarrow \quad 5000x = 4000x + 4000$$

$$\Rightarrow \quad 1000x = 4000$$

$$\Rightarrow \quad x = \dfrac{4000}{1000} = 4$$

$\therefore$ Former rate of SI = 4%.

7. $\text{SI} = \dfrac{500 \times 4 \times x}{100} = ₹\ 20x$

$$\text{Again}\quad \text{SI} = \dfrac{600 \times 3 \times x}{100} = ₹\ 18x$$

According to the question,
$$20x + 18x = 190$$
$$\Rightarrow \quad 38x = 190$$

$$\Rightarrow \quad x = \dfrac{190}{38} = 5$$

Hence rate percent in both cases = 5%

8. Let $P = ₹\ 100$

$$\text{SI} = \dfrac{P \times r \times t}{100} = \dfrac{100 \times 8 \times 5}{100}$$
$$= ₹\ 40$$
$$A = P + \text{SI} = 100 + 40$$
$$= ₹\ 140$$

when amount 140 then P = 100
when amount 1050 then P

$$= \dfrac{100}{140} \times 1050$$

$\therefore \quad P = ₹\ 750$

9. Amount after 5 years = ₹ 2000
Amount after 2 years = ₹ 1760
Interest for 3 years = 2000 − 1760
$$= ₹\ 240$$

Interest for 1 year $= \dfrac{240}{3} = ₹\ 80$

Interest for 2 years $= 80 \times 2$

$\qquad\qquad\qquad = ₹\ 160$

Principal sum = Amount after 2 years – Interest for 2 years

$\qquad = 1760 - 160 = ₹\ 1600.$

10. $SI = A - P = 2240 - 2000 = ₹\ 240$

$$t = \frac{SI \times 100}{p \times r} = \frac{240 \times 100}{2000 \times 4}$$

$$= 3 \text{ years.}$$

11. $\quad A = P\left(1 + \dfrac{r}{100}\right)^t$

$$= 8000\left(1 + \frac{5}{100}\right)^3$$

$$= 8000\left(1 + \frac{1}{20}\right)^3$$

$$= 8000\left(\frac{21}{20} \times \frac{21}{20} \times \frac{21}{20}\right)$$

$$= 9261$$

$\therefore\ C.I. = A - P = 9261 - 8000$

$$= ₹\ 1261.$$

12. $\quad A = P\left(1 + \dfrac{r}{100}\right)^t$

$$= 4000\left(1 + \frac{5}{2 \times 100}\right)^2$$

$$= 4000\left(1 + \frac{1}{40}\right)^2$$

$$= 4000 \times \frac{41}{40} \times \frac{41}{40}$$

$$= \frac{8405}{2} = ₹\ 4202.50.$$

13. $\quad A = P\left(1 + \dfrac{r}{100}\right)^t$

$$4096 = 3375\left(1 + \frac{20}{3 \times 100}\right)^t$$

$$= 3375\left(1 + \frac{1}{15}\right)^t$$

$\Rightarrow \quad \dfrac{4096}{3375} = \left(\dfrac{16}{15}\right)^t$

$\Rightarrow \quad \left(\dfrac{16}{15}\right)^3 = \left(\dfrac{16}{15}\right)^t$

$\Rightarrow \qquad t = 3 \text{ years.}$

14. $x = ₹\ 110,\ \ y = ₹\ 121$

$\therefore$ Rate of interest

$$= \left(\frac{y - x}{x} \times 100\right)\%$$

$$= \left(\frac{121 - 110}{110}\right) \times 100$$

$$= \frac{11}{110} \times 100 = 10\%$$

15. Let $\ P = ₹\ 100$

$$S.I. = \frac{P \times r \times t}{100}$$

$$= \frac{100 \times 5 \times 2}{100} = ₹\ 10$$

$$A = P\left(1 + \frac{r}{100}\right)^t$$

$$= 100\left(1 + \frac{5}{100}\right)^2$$

$$= 100 \times \frac{21}{20} \times \frac{21}{20} = \frac{441}{4}$$

$$C.I. = A - P = \frac{441}{4} - 100$$

$$= \frac{441 - 400}{4} = \frac{41}{4}$$

$$CI - SI = \frac{41}{4} - 10 = \frac{41 - 40}{4} = \frac{1}{4}$$

When difference $\dfrac{1}{4}$ then P = ₹ 100

When difference 21 then P

$$= \dfrac{100}{\dfrac{1}{4}} \times 21$$

$$\Rightarrow \quad P = 100 \times 4 \times 21 = ₹\ 8400.$$

16. Let $\quad P = ₹\ 100$

$$SI = \dfrac{100 \times 10 \times 2}{100} = ₹\ 20$$

$$CI = \left[P\left(1 + \dfrac{r}{100}\right)^t - P \right]$$

$$= \left[100\left(1 + \dfrac{10}{100}\right)^2 - 100 \right]$$

$$= 100 \times \dfrac{11}{10} \times \dfrac{11}{10} - 100$$

$$= 121 - 100 = 21$$

CI − SI = 21 − 20 = 1

When difference ₹ 1 then P = ₹ 100

When difference ₹ 8 then P

$$= 100 \times 8 = ₹\ 800$$

Hence, P = ₹ 800.

17. $\qquad A = P\left(1 + \dfrac{r}{100}\right)^t$

$$\Rightarrow 882 = 800\left(1 + \dfrac{5}{100}\right)^t$$

$$\Rightarrow \dfrac{882}{800} = \left(\dfrac{21}{20}\right)^t \Rightarrow \dfrac{441}{400} = \left(\dfrac{21}{20}\right)^t$$

$$\left(\dfrac{21}{20}\right)^2 = \left(\dfrac{21}{20}\right)^t \Rightarrow t = 2 \text{ years.}$$

18. Let the sum be P. Then,

$$1352 = P\left(1 + \dfrac{4}{100}\right)^2$$

$$\Rightarrow 1352 = \dfrac{26}{25} \times \dfrac{26}{25} P$$

$$\Rightarrow \qquad P = \dfrac{1352 \times 25 \times 25}{26 \times 26}$$

$$= ₹\ 1250.$$

19. $A = P\left(1 + \dfrac{r}{100}\right)^t$

$$\Rightarrow \qquad 900 = 625\left(1 + \dfrac{r}{100}\right)^2$$

$$\Rightarrow \qquad \dfrac{900}{625} = \left(\dfrac{100 + r}{100}\right)^2$$

$$\Rightarrow \qquad \left(\dfrac{30}{25}\right)^2 = \left(\dfrac{100 + r}{100}\right)^2$$

$$\Rightarrow \qquad \dfrac{30}{25} = \dfrac{100 + r}{100}$$

$$\Rightarrow \qquad \dfrac{6}{5} = \dfrac{100 + r}{100}$$

$$\Rightarrow 5r + 500 = 600$$

$$\Rightarrow \qquad 5r = 100$$

$$\therefore \qquad r = 20\%.$$

20. Let principal be P. Then,

$$CI = \left[P\left(1 + \dfrac{r}{100}\right)^t - P \right]$$

$$\Rightarrow 420 = \left[P\left(1 + \dfrac{10}{100}\right)^2 - P \right]$$

$$\Rightarrow 420 = \dfrac{121P}{100} - P$$

$$\Rightarrow 420 = \dfrac{121P - 100P}{100} = \dfrac{21P}{100}$$

$$\Rightarrow 21P = 420 \times 100$$

$$\Rightarrow \qquad P = \dfrac{420 \times 100}{21} = ₹\ 2000$$

$$S.I. = \dfrac{P \times r \times t}{100}$$

$$= \dfrac{2000 \times 10 \times 2}{100} = ₹\ 400.$$

8

PROFIT AND LOSS

1. A loss of 5% was suffered by selling a plot for ₹ 4085. The cost price of the plot was:
   A. ₹ 4350
   B. ₹ 4259.25
   C. ₹ 4200
   D. ₹ 4300

2. Alok bought 25 kg of rice at the rate of ₹ 6 per kg and 35 kg of rice at the rate of ₹ 7 per kg. He mixed the two and sold the mixture at the rate of ₹ 6.75 per kg. What was his gain/loss in this transaction?
   A. ₹ 16 gain
   B. ₹ 16 loss
   C. ₹ 20 gain
   D. None of these

3. A man sells 320 mangoes at the cost price of 400 mangoes. His gain percent is:
   A. 10%
   B. 25%
   C. 15%
   D. 20%

4. A person bought an article and sold it at a loss of 10%. If he had bought it for 20% less and sold it for ₹ 55 more, he would have had a profit of 40%. The C.P. of the article is:
   A. ₹ 200
   B. ₹ 225
   C. ₹ 250
   D. None of these

5. A man sells a car to his friend at 10% loss. If the friend sells it for ₹ 54000 and gain 20%, the original cost price of the car was:
   A. ₹ 25000
   B. ₹ 37500
   C. ₹ 50000
   D. ₹ 60000

6. On selling an article for ₹ 240, a trader losses 4%. In order to gain 10% he must sell that article for:
   A. ₹ 264
   B. ₹ 273.20
   C. ₹ 275
   D. ₹ 280

7. The CP of an article which is sold at a loss of 25% for ₹ 150, is:
   A. ₹ 125
   B. ₹ 175
   C. ₹ 200
   D. ₹ 225

8. A dealer professing to sell at cost price, uses a 900 gm. weight for a kilogram. His gain percent is:
   A. 10
   B. 11
   C. 9
   D. $11\dfrac{1}{9}$

9. When the price of pressure cooker was increased by 15%, its sale fell down by 15%. The effect on the money receipt was:
   A. no effect
   B. 15% decrease
   C. 7.5% increase
   D. 2.25% decrease

10. A man sells two houses at the rate of ₹ 1.995 lakh each. On one he gains 5% and on the other he

loses 5%. His gain or loss per cent in the whole transaction is:
A. 0.25% loss
B. 0.25% gain
C. 2.5% loss
D. neither loss nor gain

11. By selling 12 oranges for 1 rupee a man loses 20%. How many for a rupee should he sell to get a gain of 20%?
A. 5
B. 8
C. 10
D. 15

12. The loss incurred on selling an article for ₹ 270 is as much as the profit made after selling it at 10% profit. The CP of the article is:
A. ₹ 90
B. ₹ 110
C. ₹ 363
D. ₹ 300

13. An item costing ₹ 200 is being sold at 10% loss. If the price is further reduced by 5%, the selling price will be:
A. ₹ 179
B. ₹ 175
C. ₹ 171
D. ₹ 170

14. A trader lists his articles 20% above C.P. and allows a discount of 10% on cash payment. His gain per cent is:
A. 10%
B. 6%
C. 8%
D. 5%

15. Profit after selling a commodity for ₹ 425 is same as loss after selling it for ₹ 355. The cost of the commodity is:
A. ₹ 385
B. ₹ 390
C. ₹ 395
D. ₹ 400

16. Subhash purchased a tape recorder at $\frac{9}{10}$ th of its selling price and sold it at 8% more than its selling price. His gain is:
A. 8%
B. 10%
C. 18%
D. 20%

17. A man purchased a watch for ₹ 400 and sold it at a gain of 20% of the selling price. The selling price of the watch is:
A. ₹ 300
B. ₹ 320
C. ₹ 440
D. ₹ 500

18. By selling a table for ₹ 30 instead of ₹ 40, 5% more is lost. The cost of the table is:
A. ₹ 250
B. ₹ 210
C. ₹ 200
D. ₹ 225

19. The selling price of 12 articles is equal to the cost price of 15 articles. The gain percent is:
A. 15%
B. 25%
C. 18%
D. 35%

20. If the selling price of 10 articles is the same as the cost price of 11 articles, then find gain percent.
A. 10%
B. 15%
C. 25%
D. 20%

ANSWERS

1	2	3	4	5	6	7	8	9	10
D	D	B	C	C	C	C	D	D	A

11	12	13	14	15	16	17	18	19	20
B	D	C	C	B	D	D	C	B	A

EXPLANATORY ANSWERS

1. $100 - 5 = 95$

When SP ₹ 95 then CP = ₹ 100

When SP ₹ 4085 then CP

$$= \frac{100}{95} \times 4085 = 4300$$

∴ Cost price of the plot = ₹ 4300.

2. CP of total 60 kg of rice

$$= 6 \times 25 + 7 \times 35$$
$$= 150 + 245 = ₹ 395$$

S.P. of total 60 kg of rice

$$= 6.75 \times 60 = ₹ 405$$

Profit = $405 - 395 = ₹ 10$.

3. Let C.P. of each mango be ₹ 1

C.P. of 400 mangoes = ₹ 400

∴ C.P. of 320 mangoes = ₹ 320

S.P. of 320 mangoes = ₹ 400

Profit = $400 - 320 = 80$

$$\text{Profit \%} = \frac{\text{Profit}}{\text{CP}} \times 100$$

$$= \frac{80}{320} \times 100 = 25\%.$$

4. Let C.P. = ₹ x

$$\text{S.P.} = 90\% \text{ of } x = ₹\frac{90}{100} \times x$$

$$= ₹\frac{9x}{10}$$

$$\text{New C.P.} = 80\% \text{ of } x = ₹\frac{80}{100} \times x$$

$$= ₹\frac{4x}{5}$$

Now gain = 40%

$$∴ \text{ New S.P.} = 140\% \text{ of } \frac{4x}{5}$$

$$= ₹\frac{28x}{25}$$

Thus, $\dfrac{28x}{25} - \dfrac{9x}{10} = 55$

$$\Rightarrow \quad \frac{56x - 45x}{50} = 55$$

$$\Rightarrow \quad 11x = 55 \times 50$$

$$\Rightarrow \quad x = \frac{55 \times 50}{11} = 5 \times 50 = 250$$

∴   CP = ₹ 250.

5.   S.P. = ₹ 54000

gain = 20%

$100 + 20 = 120$

When SP ₹ 120 then CP = ₹ 100

When SP ₹ 54000 then CP

$$= \frac{100}{120} \times 54000$$

CP = ₹ 45000

Now,   SP = ₹ 45000

Loss = 10%

$100 - 10 = 90$

When SP ₹ 90 then CP = ₹ 100

When SP ₹ 45000 then CP

$$= \frac{100}{90} \times 45000$$

∴   CP = ₹ 50000.

6. $100 - 4 = 96$

When SP ₹ 96 then CP = ₹ 100

When SP ₹ 240 then CP

$$= \frac{100}{96} \times 240 = 250$$

Now, $100 + 10 = 110$

When CP ₹ 100 then SP = ₹ 110

When CP ₹ 250 then SP

$$= \frac{110}{100} \times 250 = 275$$

∴ SP = ₹ 275.

7. Loss = 25%

$\therefore$ 100 – 25 = 75

When SP ₹ 75 then CP = ₹ 100

When SP ₹ 150 then CP

$$= \frac{100}{75} \times 150$$

$\therefore$ CP = ₹ 200

8. Let the CP of 1 gm be ₹ 1 then

CP of 900 gm = ₹ 900

SP of 900 gm = CP of 1000 gm

$$= ₹ 1000$$

Profit = 1000 – 900 = ₹ 100

$$\text{gain \%} = \frac{100}{900} \times 100 = \frac{100}{9}$$

$$= 11\frac{1}{9}\% .$$

9. Let the original cost of each cooker be ₹ 1 and let the number sold originally be 100

Total sale proceed = 100 × 1

$$= ₹ 100$$

New rate = (115% of ₹ 1) = ₹ 1.15

Number sold now = 85

$\therefore$ Sale proceed now = 1.15 × 85

$$= ₹ 97.75$$

So, there is a decrease of 2.25% of money receipt.

10. In such problems, there is always a loss

$$\text{Loss\%} = \frac{(\text{Common loss and gain})^2}{10}$$

$$= \left(\frac{5}{10}\right)^2 = \frac{25}{100} = 0.25\%$$

11. SP = ₹ 1, Loss 20%

$$\Rightarrow \text{CP} = \frac{100}{80} \times 1 = ₹ \frac{5}{4}$$

gain = 20%

$$\Rightarrow \text{SP} = \frac{120}{100} \times \frac{5}{4} = ₹ \frac{3}{2}$$

For ₹ $\dfrac{3}{2}$, he must sell 12 oranges.

For ₹ 1, he must sell $\left(12 \times \dfrac{2}{3}\right)$

$$= 8 \text{ oranges.}$$

12. Let CP be ₹ x then,

$$x - 270 = 10\% \text{ of } x = \frac{x}{10}$$

$$\Rightarrow x - \frac{x}{10} = 270$$

$$\Rightarrow 9x = 2700 \Rightarrow x = 300$$

$\therefore$ Cost price = ₹ 300.

13. Loss $= \dfrac{10}{100} \times 200 = ₹ 20$

SP = CP – Loss

$$= 200 - 20 = ₹180$$

Again loss $= \dfrac{5}{100} \times 180 = ₹ 9$

$\therefore$ SP = 180 – 9 = ₹ 171.

14. Let CP = ₹ 100

then, M.P. = 100 + 20 = ₹ 120

Discount $= \dfrac{10}{100} \times 120 = ₹ 12$

S.P. = MP – dis. = 120 – 12 = 108

$\therefore$ Profit = SP – CP

$$= 108 - 100 = ₹ 8$$

$$\text{Profit\%} = \frac{\text{Profit}}{\text{CP}} \times 100$$

$$= \frac{8}{100} \times 100 = 8\%.$$

15. Let CP = ₹ x. Then,

$$425 - x = x - 355$$

$$\Rightarrow 2x = 425 + 355 = 780$$

$$\Rightarrow x = 390$$

$$\therefore \quad \text{CP} = ₹ 390.$$

16. Let S.P. = ₹ x

Then, C.P. paid by Subhash

$$= ₹ \ \frac{9x}{10}$$

S.P. received by Subhash

$$= (108\% \text{ of } x)$$

$$= \frac{108}{100} \times x = ₹ \ \frac{27x}{25}$$

$\therefore$ Gain = SP – CP

$$= \frac{27x}{25} - \frac{9x}{10}$$

$$= \frac{54x - 45x}{50} = \frac{9x}{50}$$

Hence Gain% $= \dfrac{\dfrac{9x}{50}}{\dfrac{9x}{10}} \times 100$

$$= \frac{9x}{50} \times \frac{10}{9x} \times 100$$

$$= 20\%.$$

17. Let SP = ₹ 100

Profit = 20% of SP $= \dfrac{20}{100} \times 100$

$$= ₹ \ 20$$

$\therefore$ CP = 100 – 20 = ₹ 80

When CP ₹ 80 then SP = ₹ 100

When CP ₹ 400 then SP

$$= ₹ \ \frac{100}{80} \times 400$$

SP = ₹ 500.

18. Let CP be ₹ x

if SP = ₹ 30, loss = ₹ $(x - 30)$

if SP = ₹ 40, loss = ₹ $(x - 40)$

$$\therefore (x - 30) - (x - 40) = \left(\frac{5}{100} \times x \right)$$

$$\Rightarrow 10 = \frac{5}{100} \times x$$

$$\Rightarrow \quad x = 200$$

Hence, CP = ₹ 200.

19. $15 - 12 = 3$

$$\text{Profit\%} = \frac{\text{Profit}}{\text{CP}} \times 100$$

$$= \frac{3}{12} \times 100 = 25\%$$

20. $11 - 10 = 1$

$$\text{Profit\%} = \frac{1}{10} \times 100 = 10\%.$$

9

PERCENTAGE

1. If 90% of A = 30% of B and B = x% of A, then the value of x is:
   - A. 600
   - B. 800
   - C. 300
   - D. 900

2. In an examination, 52% of the candidates failed in English, 42% failed in mathematics and 17% failed in both. The number of those who have passed in both the subjects is:
   - A. 23%
   - B. 35%
   - C. 25%
   - D. 40%

3. The price of cooking oil has increased by 25%. The percentage of reduction that a family should effect in the use of cooking oil so as not to increase the expenditure on this account is:
   - A. 15%
   - B. 20%
   - C. 25%
   - D. 30%

4. A man received 10% increase in his salary. His new salary is ₹ 5060. His original salary was:
   - A. ₹ 4554
   - B. ₹ 4600
   - C. ₹ 4200
   - D. ₹ 4400

5. If x is 90% of y, what per cent of x is y?
   - A. 90
   - B. 190
   - C. 101.1
   - D. 111.1

6. The population of a town increases by 5% annually. If it is 15435 now, its population 2 years ago was:
   - A. 14000
   - B. 15000
   - C. 10620
   - D. 13000

7. In an examination 93% of students passed and 259 failed. The total number of students is:
   - A. 3200
   - B. 3700
   - C. 4100
   - D. 3900

8. The price of sugar is increased by 20%. If the expenditure is not allowed to increase, the ratio between the reduction in consumption and original consumption is:
   - A. $\dfrac{1}{5}$
   - B. $\dfrac{1}{3}$
   - C. $\dfrac{1}{6}$
   - D. $\dfrac{1}{7}$

9. A mixture of 40 litres of milk and water contains 10% water. How much water should be added to this so that water may be 20% in the new mixture?
   - A. 2 l
   - B. 3 l
   - C. 4 l
   - D. 5 l

10. The side of a square is increased by 25%, then how much per cent does its area get increased?
    - A. 56.25
    - B. 50
    - C. 125
    - D. 156.25

11. Which number is 60% less than 80?

A. 48   B. 42
C. 32   D. 12

12. In an examination 70% candidates passed in English and 65% in Mathematics. If 27% candidates failed in both the subjects and 248 passed the examination, the total number of candidates was:

A. 400   B. 348
C. 420   D. 484

13. Rajan spends 86% of his monthly income. He saves ₹ 1050 per month. His monthly income is:

A. ₹ 5000   B. ₹ 8000
C. ₹ 7500   D. ₹ 6500

14. In an election between two candidates, the candidate who gets 30% of the votes polled is defeated by 15000 votes. The number of votes polled by the winning candidate is:

A. 13250   B. 26250
C. 32000   D. 16000

15. If the diameter of a circle is increased by 100%, its area is increased by:

A. 100%   B. 200%
C. 300%   D. 400%

16. At an election, a candidate secures 40% of the votes but is defeated by the other candidate by a majority of 298 votes. The total number of votes recorded were:

A. 1490   B. 1280
C. 1360   D. 1540

17. A owns a house worth ₹ 10000, he sells it to B at a profit of 10% based on the worth of the house. B sells the house back to A at a loss of 10%. In this transaction, A gets:

A. a profit of ₹ 2000
B. a profit of ₹ 1100
C. a profit of ₹ 1000
D. no profit no loss

18. The price of an article is cut by 10%. To restore it to the former value, the new price must be increased by

A. 10%   B. $9\frac{1}{11}\%$

C. $11\frac{1}{9}\%$ D. 11%

19. P is six times as large as q. The percent that q is less than P, is:

A. $16\frac{2}{3}$ B. 60

C. 90   D. $83\frac{1}{3}$

20. If 10% of m is the same as 20% of n then $m : n$ is equal to:

A. 1 : 2   B. 2 : 1
C. 5 : 1   D. 10 : 1

ANSWERS

1	2	3	4	5	6	7	8	9	10
C	A	B	B	D	A	B	C	D	A

11	12	13	14	15	16	17	18	19	20
C	A	C	B	C	A	B	C	D	B

EXPLANATORY ANSWERS

1. $\dfrac{90}{100}A = \dfrac{30}{100}B = \dfrac{30}{100} \times \dfrac{x}{100}A$

$\therefore\ x = \dfrac{90}{100} \times \dfrac{100 \times 100}{30} = 300.$

2. Failed in English only
$= (52 - 17)\% = 35\%$
Failed in Mathematics only
$= (42 - 17)\% = 25\%$
Failed in both $= 17\%$
Failed $= (35 + 25 + 17)\% = 77\%$
$\therefore$ Passed in both the subjects
$= (100 - 77)\% = 23\%.$

3. Reduction in consumption

$= \left(\dfrac{25}{125} \times 100\right)\% = 20\%.$

4. If new salary is ₹ 110, original salary $= 100$
If new salary is ₹ 5060, original

salary $= \dfrac{100}{110} \times 5060 = ₹\ 4600.$

5. $x = 90\%$ of $y = \dfrac{90}{100} \times y = \dfrac{9y}{10}$

$\Rightarrow \dfrac{y}{x} = \dfrac{10}{9}$

Let $y = z\%$ of $x = \dfrac{z}{100}x$

$\Rightarrow \dfrac{y}{x} = \dfrac{z}{100}$

$\therefore\ \dfrac{z}{100} = \dfrac{10}{9} \Rightarrow 9z = 1000$

$z = \dfrac{1000}{9} = 111.1\%.$

6. Let the population two years ago be x.

Then, $x\left(1 + \dfrac{5}{100}\right)^2 = 15435$

$\Rightarrow\ x\left(\dfrac{21 \times 21}{20 \times 20}\right) = 15435$

$\Rightarrow\ x = \dfrac{20 \times 20 \times 15435}{21 \times 21} = 14000$

7. Let total number of students $= x$.
93% of $x + 259 = x$

$\Rightarrow \dfrac{93}{100}x + 259 = x$

$\Rightarrow\ x - \dfrac{93}{100}x = 259$

$\Rightarrow\ 7x = 100 \times 259$

$\Rightarrow\ x = \dfrac{100 \times 259}{7}$

$= 37 \times 100 = 3700.$

8. Reduction in consumption

$= \left[\dfrac{r}{100 + r} \times 100\right]\%$

$= \left(\dfrac{20}{120} \times 100\right)\% = \dfrac{50}{3}\%$

$\therefore\ \dfrac{\text{Reduction in consumption}}{\text{Original consumption}}$

$= \dfrac{50}{3 \times 100} = \dfrac{1}{6}.$

9. Milk in 40 litres $= 90\%$ of 40

$= \dfrac{90}{100} \times 40 = 36$ litres

Let x litres of water be added to it.

Then, $\dfrac{4+x}{40+x} \times 100 = 20$

$\Rightarrow \dfrac{4+x}{40+x} = \dfrac{1}{5}$

$\Rightarrow 20 + 5x = 40 + x$

$\Rightarrow \qquad x = 5$ litres.

10. Let original side = 100 units.
Then, new side = 125 units
Increase in area
$= [(125)^2 - (100)^2]$
$= (125 + 100)(125 - 100)$
$= 225 \times 25 = 5625$
$\therefore$ Percentage increase

$$= \left(\dfrac{5625}{100 \times 100} \times 100 \right) \%$$

$$= 56.25\%$$

11. $80 - 60\%$ of $80 = 80 - \dfrac{60}{100} \times 80$

$$= 80 - 48 = 32.$$

12. Failed in English only
$= (30 - 27)\% = 3\%$
Failed in Mathematics only
$= (35 - 27) = 8\%$
Failed in both the subjects $= 27\%$
Failed in one or both of the subjects $= (3 + 8 + 27)\% = 38\%$
$\therefore 62\%$ of $x = 248$

$\Rightarrow \dfrac{62}{100} \times x = 248$

$\Rightarrow \qquad x = \dfrac{248 \times 100}{62}$

$$= 4 \times 100 = 400$$

Hence, total number of candidates
$= 400$.

13. Let Rajan's monthly income $= ₹\ x$
14% of $x = 1050$

$\Rightarrow \dfrac{14}{100} \times x = 1050$

$\Rightarrow \qquad x = \dfrac{100 \times 1050}{14}$

$$= 100 \times 75 = 7500$$

Hence, Rajan's monthly income
$= ₹\ 7500$.

14. 70% of $x - 30\%$ of $x = 15000$

$\Rightarrow 40\%$ of $x = 15000$

$\Rightarrow \dfrac{40}{100} \times x = 15000$

$\Rightarrow x = \dfrac{15000 \times 100}{40} = 26250$

Hence total votes poled $= 26250$.

15. Let diameter $= 100$ m
New diameter $= 200$ m
Change in area
$= \pi \times (100)^2 - \pi \times (50)^2$
$= \pi\ [100^2 - 50^2]$
$= \pi\ (100 + 50)\ (100 - 50)$
$= \pi\ (150 \times 50) = 7500\pi$
$\therefore$ Percentage increase

$$= \dfrac{7500\pi}{\pi \times 50 \times 50} \times 100 = 300\%.$$

16. 60% of $x - 40\%$ of $x = 298$

$\Rightarrow 20\%$ of $x = 298$

$\Rightarrow \dfrac{20}{100} \times x = 298$

$\Rightarrow \dfrac{x}{5} = 298$

$\Rightarrow x = 5 \times 298 = 1490.$

17. Price paid by B $= ₹\ \dfrac{110}{100} \times 10000$

$$= ₹\ 11000$$

Price paid by A $= ₹\ \dfrac{90}{100} \times 11000$

$$= ₹\ 9900$$

Thus profit made by A in two transactions
$$= ₹(1000 + 100) = ₹\ 1100.$$

18. Let the original price = ₹ 100
Reduced price = ₹ 90
Increment on ₹ 90 = ₹ 10
Increment on ₹ 100
$$= \left(\frac{10}{90} \times 100\right)\%$$
$$= \frac{100}{9} = 11\frac{1}{9}\% .$$

19. $p = 6q \Rightarrow q = \dfrac{1}{6}p$

$\therefore$ q is less than p by $\left(p - \dfrac{1}{6}p\right)$

$$= \frac{5p}{6}$$

$\therefore$ Required percentage

$$= \left(\frac{5p}{6} \times \frac{1}{p} \times 100\right)$$

$$= \frac{250}{3} = 83\frac{1}{3}\% .$$

20. $\dfrac{10}{100}m = \dfrac{20}{100}n$

$\Rightarrow \quad \dfrac{m}{10} = \dfrac{n}{5}$

$\Rightarrow \quad \dfrac{m}{n} = \dfrac{10}{5} = \dfrac{2}{1}$

$\therefore$ $m : n = 2 : 1.$

10

SPEED, TIME AND DISTANCE

1. A train crosses a pole in 10 seconds. If the length of the train is 150 m, then what is the speed of the train?
   A. 54 km/hr
   B. 60 km/hr
   C. 72 km/hr
   D. 45 km/hr

2. A train 160 m long crosses a platform of 160 m length in 16 seconds. What is the speed of the train?
   A. 68 km/hr
   B. 70 km/hr
   C. 72 km/hr
   D. 62 km/hr

3. Two trains are running towards each other at the speed of 40 km/hr and 30 km/hr respectively on parallel lines. If the distance between two trains is 105 km, then after how much time they will meet each other?
   A. $1\dfrac{1}{3}$ hr
   B. $1\dfrac{1}{2}$ hr
   C. 2 hr
   D. $1\dfrac{1}{4}$ hr

4. A train whose length is 120 m, crosses a bridge in 12 seconds at a speed of 60 km/hr. What is the length of the bridge?
   A. 75 m
   B. 80 m
   C. 85 m
   D. 90 m

5. A boat in the direction of flow covers a distance of 60 km in 4 hours. If speed of the boat is double the speed of flow then how much distance it covers in 2 hours opposite the flow?
   A. 10 km
   B. 8 km
   C. 11 km
   D. 15 km

6. A train running at a speed of 54 km/hr passes a man standing on the platform is 9 seconds. Length of the train in metre is:
   A. 140 m
   B. 135 m
   C. 145 m
   D. 120 m

7. A train 110 m long is moving at a speed of 130 km/hr. How long will it take to pass a platform 165 m long?
   A. $8\dfrac{9}{13}$ seconds
   B. $7\dfrac{9}{13}$ seconds
   C. $7\dfrac{8}{13}$ seconds
   D. $7\dfrac{8}{11}$ seconds

8. A car moving at 48 km/hr completes a journey in 10 hours. By how much the speed of this car should be increased so as to do this journey in 8 hours?
   A. 8 km/hr
   B. 12 km/hr
   C. 10 km/hr
   D. 15 km/hr

9. Starting from a point at a speed of 4 km/hr a man reaches at a certain place and returns back to the point from where he had started journey on bicycle at the speed of 16 km/hr. His average speed during the entire journey will be:
   A. 6.4 km/hr
   B. 8.4 km/hr
   C. 5.4 km/hr
   D. 10 km/hr

10. A motorist covers a certain distance at an average speed of 48 km/hr in 45 minutes. What speed in km/hr he must maintain to cover the same distance in 30 minutes?
    A. 66 km/hr
    B. 79 km/hr
    C. 80 km/hr
    D. 72 km/hr

11. A train 180 m long is running at a speed of 42 km/hr. In what time it crosses a man going at a speed of 6 km/hr in the same direction?
    A. 11 seconds
    B. 21 seconds
    C. 23 seconds
    D. 18 seconds

12. A man travels a distance of 6 km at a speed of 4 km/hr and a distance of 4 km at a speed of 3 km/hr. What is his average speed in total journey?
    A. $3\frac{9}{17}$ km/hr
    B. $4\frac{9}{17}$ km/hr
    C. $2\frac{1}{17}$ km/hr
    D. $3\frac{1}{17}$ km/hr

13. A man travels a distance at a speed of 8 km/hr and returns at a speed of 6 km/hr. If he takes $3\frac{1}{2}$ hr time in total journey, then how much distance he covered?
    A. 25 km
    B. 28 km
    C. 24 km
    D. 30 km

14. The circumference of a motor wheel is $4\frac{2}{7}$ m. The wheel completes 7 rounds in 4 seconds. What is the speed (in km/hr) of the motor?
    A. 22
    B. 27
    C. 30
    D. 31

15. A certain distance is covered at a certain speed. If half the distance is covered in double time, then what is the ratio of two speeds?
    A. 4 : 1
    B. 4 : 3
    C. 3 : 1
    D. 1 : 4

16. A and B start walking at the same time on a circular path with circumference 35 metre. If they walk in the same direction at 4 km/hr and 5 km/hr respectively, after what time will they meet together?
    A. 35 hrs
    B. 27 hrs
    C. 24 hrs
    D. 40 hrs

17. While walking at $\frac{3}{5}$ of his usual speed Sonu reaches at his destination late by 30 minutes. His usual time consumed in reaching to his destination is:
    A. 32 min
    B. 40 min
    C. 45 min
    D. 42 min

18. Two trains 150 m long and 100 m long are running in opposite directions on parallel lines at 50 km/hr and 70 km/hr respectively. How long does it take to pass each other?

A. $7\dfrac{1}{2}$ seconds

B. $8\dfrac{1}{3}$ seconds

C. $7\dfrac{3}{4}$ seconds

D. $8\dfrac{3}{4}$ seconds

19. The speed of a boat in still water is 8 km/hr. If it can travel 12 km upstream at the same time as it can travel 120 km downstream,

the rate of flow of stream in km/hr is:

A. 4 km/hr   B. 2 km/hr

C. 4.5 km/hr   D. 5.5 km/hr

20. Kanchan walks from her home at 4 km/hr and reaches her school 5 minutes late. If she walks at 5 km/hr, she reaches the school $2\dfrac{1}{2}$ minutes earlier. How far is the school from her home?

A. 3.5 km   B. 2.5 km

C. 2.75 km   D. 3.2 km

ANSWERS

1	2	3	4	5	6	7	8	9	10
A	C	B	B	A	B	C	B	A	D

11	12	13	14	15	16	17	18	19	20
D	A	C	B	A	A	C	A	B	B

EXPLANATORY ANSWERS

1. $\because$ The train crosses the pole. So in given time it covers the distance equal to its length.

$\therefore$ Speed of the train $= \dfrac{\text{Distance}}{\text{Time}}$

$= \dfrac{150}{10} = 15$ m/s

$= 15 \times \dfrac{18}{5}$ km/hr

$= 3 \times 18 = 54$ km/hr

2. $\because$ The train crosses the platform

$\therefore$ Distance covered by the train

= length of the train + length of the platform

= 160 + 160 = 320 m,

time = 16 seconds

Speed of the train $= \dfrac{\text{Distance}}{\text{Time}}$

$= \dfrac{320}{16} = 20$ m/s

$= 20 \times \dfrac{18}{5} = 72$ km/hr.

3. Two trains are moving towards each other

$\therefore$ Relative speed = 40 + 30

= 70 km/hr

Distance = 105 km

Time $= \dfrac{\text{Distance}}{\text{Speed}} = \dfrac{105}{70} = \dfrac{3}{2}$ hrs

$= 1\dfrac{1}{2}$ hrs.

$\therefore$ Trains meet each other after $1\dfrac{1}{2}$ hrs.

4. Let the length of the bridge = x metres

Distance covered by train
= length of the train + length of the bridge = $(120 + x)$m

Time = 12 seconds

$$\text{Speed} = \frac{\text{Distance}}{\text{Time}}$$

$$= \frac{(120 + x)}{12} \text{ m/s}$$

$$= \frac{(120 + x)}{12} \times \frac{18}{5} \text{ km/hr}$$

But speed of the train = 60 km/hr
(given)

$$\therefore \quad \frac{120 + x}{12} \times \frac{18}{5} = 60$$

$$(120 + x) = \frac{12 \times 5 \times 60}{18} = 200$$

$$\Rightarrow x = 200 - 120 = 80$$

$\therefore$ Length of the bridge = 80 m.

5. In the direction of flow:

$$\text{Speed of the boat} = \frac{60}{4}$$

$$= 15 \text{ km/hr}$$

$\therefore$ Speed of the boat in still water + Speed of flow = 15 km/hr

According to the problem,

Speed of the boat in still water
= 2 × speed of flow

$\therefore$ 3 × speed of the flow = 15 km/hr

$$\therefore \text{ Speed of flow} = \frac{15}{3} = 5 \text{ km/hr}$$

Speed of the boat in still water
= 15 − 5 = 10 km/hr

Against the flow:

Distance covered by boat in 2 hrs
= (Speed of boat in still water
− speed of flow) × 2
= (10 − 5) × 2 = 5 × 2 = 10 km.

6. Here, the train has to cover a distance equal to its length.

Speed of the train = 54 km/hr

$$= 54 \times \frac{5}{18} \text{ m/s} = 15 \text{ m/s}$$

$\therefore$ Length of the train
= Speed × time = 15 × 9
= 135 metres.

7. In this case the train will cover the distance equal to its own length plus length of the platform.

Distance covered by the train
= 110 + 165 = 275 m

Speed of the train = 130 km/hr

$$= 130 \times \frac{5}{18} = \frac{325}{9} \text{ m/s}$$

Time taken to pass the platform

$$= \frac{275}{\dfrac{325}{9}} = \frac{275 \times 9}{325} = \frac{99}{13}$$

$$= 7\frac{8}{13} \text{ Seconds.}$$

8. Distance covered by the car in 10 hrs at 48 km/hr = 48 × 10 = 480 km

Again, distance = 480 km,
time = 8 hrs

$$\therefore \text{ Speed of the car} = \frac{480}{8}$$

$$= 60 \text{ km/hr}$$

Hence, increase that should be effected in the speed of the car
= 60 − 48 = 12 km/hr.

9. Distance covered by the man in the two cases are equal.

Here, a = 4 km/hr, b = 16 km/hr

Average speed during the entire journey

$$= \frac{2ab}{a+b} = \frac{2 \times 4 \times 16}{4+16}$$

$$= \frac{2 \times 4 \times 16}{20} = \frac{64}{10}$$

$$= 6.4 \text{ km/hr.}$$

10. Distance covered by the motorist in 45 minutes at 48 km/hr

$$= 48 \times \frac{45}{60} = 12 \times 3 = 36 \text{ km}$$

Now, Distance = 36 km

$$\text{Time} = 30 \text{ min.} = \frac{1}{2} \text{ hrs}$$

$\therefore$ Speed of the motorist

$$= \frac{\text{Distance}}{\text{Time}} = \frac{36}{\dfrac{1}{2}}$$

$$= 36 \times 2 = 72 \text{ km/hr.}$$

11. $\because$ Train and man are travelling in same direction

$\therefore$ Resulting speed = 42 – 6

$$= 36 \text{ km/hr}$$

$$= 36 \times \frac{5}{18} \text{ m/s} = 10 \text{ m/s}$$

Distance covered = 180 m

$$\therefore \text{Time} = \frac{\text{Distance}}{\text{Speed}} = \frac{180}{10}$$

$$= 18 \text{ seconds.}$$

12. Time required to cover a distance of 6 km at a speed of 4 km/hr

$$= \frac{6}{4} = \frac{3}{2} \text{ hrs}$$

Time required to cover a distance of 4 km at a speed of 3 km/hr

$$= \frac{4}{3} \text{ hrs}$$

$$\text{Total time} = \frac{3}{2} + \frac{4}{3} = \frac{9+8}{6}$$

$$= \frac{17}{6} \text{ hrs}$$

Total distance = 6 + 4 = 10 km

$$\therefore \text{Average speed} = \frac{\text{Total distance}}{\text{Toral time}}$$

$$= \frac{10}{\dfrac{17}{6}} = \frac{10 \times 6}{17}$$

$$= \frac{60}{17} = 3\frac{9}{17} \text{ km/hr.}$$

13. Let one side distance = x km

Time required to cover a distance of x kilometer at a speed of 8 km/hr

$$= \frac{x}{8} \text{ hr}$$

Time required to cover a distance of x km at a speed of 6 km/hr

$$= \frac{x}{6} \text{ hr}$$

$$\text{Total time} = 3\frac{1}{2} \text{ hr (given)}$$

$$\therefore \quad \frac{x}{8} + \frac{x}{6} = \frac{7}{2}$$

$$\Rightarrow \frac{3x+4x}{24} = \frac{7}{2} \Rightarrow \frac{7x}{24} = \frac{7}{2}$$

$$\Rightarrow x = 12$$

$\therefore$ Total distance = 12 + 12

$$= 24 \text{ km.}$$

14. Circumference of the wheel

$$= 4\frac{2}{7} \text{ m} = \frac{30}{7} \text{ m}$$

Distance covered by the wheel in

$$\text{one round} = \frac{30}{7} \text{ m}$$

$\therefore$ Distance covered by the wheel in 7 rounds

$$= \frac{30 \times 7}{7} = 30 \text{ m}$$

According to problem, this distance is covered in 4 seconds

$$\therefore \text{ Speed} = \frac{\text{Distance}}{\text{Time}} = \frac{30}{4} \text{ m/s}$$

$$= \frac{30}{4} \times \frac{18}{5} = 27 \text{ km/hr}$$

$\therefore$ Speed of the motor = 27 km/hr.

15. Let distance = x and speed = V_1

$$\therefore \text{ time } (t) = \frac{x}{V_1} \Rightarrow V_1 = \frac{x}{t}$$

According to the problem,

$$\text{Distance} = \frac{x}{2} \text{ and time} = 2t$$

$$\therefore \text{ Speed } (V_2) = \frac{x/2}{2t} = \frac{x}{4t}$$

$$\therefore \frac{V_1}{V_2} = \frac{x/t}{x/4t} = \frac{4}{1}$$

$$\Rightarrow V_1 : V_2 = 4 : 1$$

16. The two persons walk in the same direction

$\therefore$ Their relative speed = 5 – 4

$$= 1 \text{ km/hr}$$

Distance covered in 1 round on the circular path = 35 km

$$\therefore \text{ They will meet after } \frac{35}{1}$$

$$= 35 \text{ hrs.}$$

17. Let usual speed of Sonu is V km/hr and his destination is at a distance of x km.

$\therefore$ Usual time of arrival at the

$$\text{destination} = \frac{x}{V} \text{ hrs} \qquad ...(i)$$

Time taken in covering x km at $\dfrac{3}{5}$ V km/hr

$$= \frac{x}{3V/5} = \frac{5x}{3V} \text{ hrs}$$

$\therefore$ Usual time of arrival

$$= \left(\frac{5x}{3V} - \frac{30}{60} \right) \text{ hrs} \qquad ...(ii)$$

From equation (i) and (ii),

$$\frac{x}{V} = \frac{5x}{3V} - \frac{1}{2} \Rightarrow \frac{5x}{3V} - \frac{x}{V} = \frac{1}{2}$$

$$\Rightarrow \frac{2x}{3V} = \frac{1}{2} \Rightarrow 4x = 3V$$

$$\Rightarrow \frac{x}{V} = \frac{3}{4} \text{ hrs}$$

Therefore, it is clear that usual time of arrival at the destination

$$= \frac{3}{4} \text{ hrs}$$

$$= \frac{3}{4} \times 60 = 3 \times 15 = 45 \text{ minutes.}$$

18. The two trains are running in opposite directions

$\therefore$ Relative speed = 50 + 70

$$= 120 \text{ km/hr}$$

$$= 120 \times \frac{5}{18} \text{ m/s}$$

And distance covered by the train

$$= 150 + 100 = 250 \text{ m}$$

$\therefore$ Time taken to pass each other

$$= \dfrac{250}{120 \times \dfrac{5}{18}} = \dfrac{250 \times 18}{120 \times 5}$$

$$= \dfrac{15}{2} = 7\dfrac{1}{2} \text{ seconds.}$$

19. Let the boat covers the distance in each of the two cases in t hrs.

In the first case:

Against the stream: Speed of the boat $= \dfrac{12}{t}$ km/hr

$\therefore$ Speed of the boat in still water
$\qquad$ − speed of the current

$$= \dfrac{12}{t} \text{ km/hr} \qquad ...(i)$$

In the second case:

Down the stream: Speed of the boat $= \dfrac{20}{t}$ km/hr

Speed of the boat in still water
$\qquad$ + speed of the current

$$= \dfrac{20}{t} \text{ km/hr} \qquad ...(ii)$$

From (i) and (ii),

2 × speed of the boat in still water

$$= \dfrac{12}{t} + \dfrac{20}{t} = \dfrac{32}{t} \text{ km/hr}$$

But speed of the boat in still water
$\qquad$ = 8 km/hr (given)

$$\therefore \quad 2 \times 8 = \dfrac{32}{t} \Rightarrow t = \dfrac{32}{16} = 2$$

From equation (i),

$$8 - \text{speed of the current} = \dfrac{12}{2} = 6$$

$\therefore$ Speed of the current = 8 − 6
$$= 2 \text{ km/hr.}$$

20. Let the distance between her house to the school = x km

$\therefore$ Time spent in covering x km at the rate of 4 km/hr = $\dfrac{x}{4}$ hrs

But Kanchan reaches her school late 5 min.

$\therefore$ Usual time for reaching the school $= \dfrac{x}{4}$ hrs − 5 min.

$$= \left(\dfrac{x}{4} - \dfrac{1}{12} \right) \text{ hrs}$$

And time spent in covering x km at 5 km/hr $= \dfrac{x}{5}$ hrs

But this time Kanchan reaches her school $2\dfrac{1}{2}$ minutes earlier.

Usual time of reaching the school

$$= \dfrac{x}{5} \text{ hrs} + 2\dfrac{1}{2} \text{ min}$$

$$= \left(\dfrac{x}{5} + \dfrac{1}{24} \right) \text{ hrs}$$

$$\dfrac{x}{4} - \dfrac{1}{12} = \dfrac{x}{5} + \dfrac{1}{24}$$

$$\Rightarrow \dfrac{x}{4} - \dfrac{x}{5} = \dfrac{1}{12} + \dfrac{1}{24}$$

$$\Rightarrow \dfrac{x}{20} = \dfrac{1}{8} \quad \Rightarrow 8x = 20$$

$$\Rightarrow x = \dfrac{20}{8} = 2.5 \text{ km}$$

Therefore, her school is at a distance of 2.5 km from her home.

11

TIME, WORK AND WAGES

1. 12 boys can do a piece of work in 16 days. In how many days can 6 boys do the same work?
   A. 16 days   B. 32 days
   C. 23 days   D. 24 days

2. A can do a piece of work in 8 days while B can do the same work in 16 days. If they start working together, how long would they take to complete half portion of this work?

   A. $2\frac{2}{3}$ days   B. $3\frac{5}{7}$ days

   C. $4\frac{1}{2}$ days   D. $3\frac{1}{2}$ days

3. A can do a piece of work in 4 days. B is 50% more efficient than A. How long would B alone take to complete it.

   A. $3\frac{1}{3}$ days   B. $5\frac{1}{4}$ days

   C. $2\frac{2}{3}$ days   D. $1\frac{2}{3}$ days

4. A and B working together complete a work in 35 days. If A takes 60 days to complete it, how long would B alone take to complete it?
   A. 64 days   B. 72 days
   C. 81 days   D. 84 days

5. 10 men or 18 boys can do a piece of work in 15 days. In how many days would 25 men and 15 boys complete the same work working together?

   A. $5\frac{1}{2}$ days   B. $4\frac{1}{2}$ days

   C. $6\frac{2}{3}$ days   D. $2\frac{1}{3}$ days

6. A can do $\frac{1}{2}$ of a work in 9 days while B can do $\frac{1}{3}$ of the same work in 6 days. How long would take for A and B together to complete the work?
   A. 18 days   B. 6 days
   C. 12 days   D. 9 days

7. A, B and C can complete a work separately in 24, 36 and 48 days respectively. They started together but C left after 4 days of start and A left 3 days before the completion of work. In how many days will the work be completed?
   A. 15 days   B. 18 days
   C. 10 days   D. 12 days

8. 5 men and 2 boys together in 1 hour do 4 times work as 1 man and 1 boy do in an hour.

Determine the ratio of the specified times of works of a man and a boy.

A. 4 : 1   B. 1 : 4
C. 3 : 4   D. 2 : 1

9. 75 boys finish a work in 24 days. How many men will complete twice the work in 20 days while 2 men do in a day same work as 3 boys do in a day?

A. 50   B. 120
C. 60   D. 24

10. Savita can do a piece of work in 20 days. Tripti is 25% more efficient than Savita. The number of days taken by Tripti to do the same piece of work is:

A. 15 days   B. 16 days
C. 18 days   D. 25 days

11. A, B and C together contracted to do a work for ₹ 450. If ratio of their work is 9 : 5 : 4 respectively, then find the share of A.

A. ₹ 220   B. ₹ 225
C. ₹ 325   D. ₹ 180

12. A can do a work in 16 days. If B's speed is double than A, then in how many days they together can do the work?

A. $5\frac{1}{3}$ days   B. $3\frac{1}{4}$ days

C. $4\frac{1}{3}$ days   D. $2\frac{1}{4}$ days

13. A and B together can do a work in 28 days. They finish the work with the help of C in 21 days. In how many days C alone can do the work?

A. 83 days   B. 84 days
C. 90 days   D. 45 days

14. Sapna and Sandhya can do a work in 12 days and 10 days respectively. If they work on alternative days and Sapna begins the work then in how many days the work will be completed?

A. 8 days   B. 11 days
C. 14 days   D. 5 days

15. A takes halftime than B to do a work. C takes time equal to A and B together. If three together can do the work in 7 days then in how many days A alone can do the work?

A. 21 days   B. 10 days
C. 8 days   D. 24 days

16. Working 7 hours daily 24 men can complete a piece of work in 27 days. In how many days would 14 men complete the same piece of work working 9 hours daily?

A. 32 days   B. 31 days
C. 36 days   D. 39 days

17. A, B and C undertake to do a piece of work for ₹ 529. If A and B working together do $\frac{19}{23}$ work and B and C working together do $\frac{8}{23}$ work, how should the money be divided among them?

A. ₹ 345, ₹ 102, ₹ 82
B. ₹ 345, ₹ 92, ₹ 92
C. ₹ 330, ₹ 107, ₹ 92
D. ₹ 330, ₹ 92, ₹ 107

18. Two men undertake to do a piece of work for ₹ 1400. First man alone can do this work in 7 days while the second man alone can do this work in 8 days. If they working together complete this work in 3 days with the help of a boy, how should money be divided?
A. ₹ 600, ₹ 500, ₹ 300
B. ₹ 600, ₹ 525, ₹ 275
C. ₹ 600, ₹ 550, ₹ 250
D. ₹ 500, ₹ 525, ₹ 375

19. 3 men and 5 women can do a piece of work in 8 days and 2 men and 7 boys can do the same work in 12 days. Find the number of boys if the work is done by 10 women.
A. 19 boys   B. 21 boys
C. 23 boys   D. 15 boys

20. A, B and C can complete a piece of work in 20, 12 and 18 days respectively. They start the work together but A drops out after 4 days and B drops out 2 days before the completion of work. The work is finished in :

A. $2\dfrac{22}{25}$ days   B. $6\dfrac{24}{29}$ days

C. $5\dfrac{24}{25}$ days   D. $6\dfrac{24}{25}$ days

ANSWERS

1	2	3	4	5	6	7	8	9	10
B	A	C	D	B	D	A	D	B	B

11	12	13	14	15	16	17	18	19	20
B	A	B	B	A	C	B	B	B	D

EXPLANATORY ANSWERS

1. 12 boys can do a piece of work in 16 days
1 boy can do this work in 16 × 12 days
6 boys can do this work in

$$\dfrac{16 \times 12}{6} \text{ days} = 32 \text{ days.}$$

2. Here, $x = 8$, $y = 16$
They both working together would complete $\dfrac{1}{2}$ work in

$$= \dfrac{1}{2} \times \left(\dfrac{xy}{x+y}\right) \text{ days}$$

$$= \dfrac{1}{2} \times \left(\dfrac{8 \times 16}{8+16}\right) = \dfrac{1}{2}\left(\dfrac{128}{24}\right)$$

$$= \dfrac{8}{3} \text{ days} = 2\dfrac{2}{3} \text{ days.}$$

3. A does the work in 4 days

∴ B will do this work in $4 \times \dfrac{100}{150}$

$$\text{days} = \dfrac{8}{3} \text{ days} = 2\dfrac{2}{3} \text{ days.}$$

4. Let B alone would take y days to complete this work.

Here $x = 60$

According to the question,

A and B working together complete this work in 35 days

$\Rightarrow \dfrac{xy}{x+y} = 35 \Rightarrow \dfrac{60 \times y}{60 + y} = 35$

$\Rightarrow 60y = 35 \times 60 + 35y$

$\Rightarrow 25y = 35 \times 60$

$\Rightarrow y = \dfrac{35 \times 60}{25} = 7 \times 12 = 84$

Therefore, B alone would complete this work in 84 days.

5. According to question,

Work done by 10 men = work done by 18 boys

Work done by 25 men = work done by 45 boys

$\therefore$ Work done by (25 men + 15 boys) = Work done by 45 + 15

= 60 boys

$\because$ 18 boys complete a work in 15 days

1 boy complete this work in 15 × 18 days

60 boys complete this work in

$\dfrac{15 \times 18}{60} = \dfrac{9}{2}$ days $= 4\dfrac{1}{2}$ days

Therefore, 25 men and 15 boys working together would complete

the work in $4\dfrac{1}{2}$ days.

6. A's 9 day's work $= \dfrac{1}{2}$

A's 1 day work $= \dfrac{1}{2 \times 9} = \dfrac{1}{18}$

B's 6 day's work $= \dfrac{1}{3}$

B's 1 day work $= \dfrac{1}{3 \times 6} = \dfrac{1}{18}$

(A + B)'s 1 day work $= \dfrac{1}{18} + \dfrac{1}{18}$

$= \dfrac{2}{18} = \dfrac{1}{9}$

$\therefore$ A and B both together will complete the work in 9 days.

7. Let the work be completed in x days.

Therefore, A worked for $(x - 3)$ days

B worked for x days

and   C worked for 4 days

A's 1 day work $= \dfrac{1}{24}$

B's 1 day work $= \dfrac{1}{36}$

C's 1 day work $= \dfrac{1}{48}$

$(x - 3) \times \dfrac{1}{24} + x \times \dfrac{1}{36} + 4 \times \dfrac{1}{48} = 1$

$\Rightarrow \dfrac{x-3}{24} + \dfrac{x}{36} + \dfrac{1}{12} = 1$

$\Rightarrow \dfrac{3x - 9 + 2x + 6}{72} = 1$

$\Rightarrow 5x - 3 = 72$

$\Rightarrow 5x = 75 \Rightarrow x = 15$

Hence the work was completed in 15 days.

8. Work of (5 men + 2 boys)

= 4 (work of 1 man + 1 boy)

Work of 4 men + 4 boys

$\Rightarrow$ Work of (5 men – 4 men)

= Work of (4 boys – 2 boys)

$\Rightarrow$ Work of 1 man = work of 2 boys

$\therefore$ Required ratio = 2 : 1

9. Work of 3 boys = Work of 2 men

Work of 1 boy = Work of $\dfrac{2}{3}$ man

$\therefore$ Work of 75 boys = work of

$\dfrac{2}{3} \times 75 = 50$ men

$\because$ 1 work is completed in 24 days by 50 men

$\therefore$ 1 work is completed in 1 day by 50×24 men

$\therefore$ 2 work are completed in 20 days by

$$\dfrac{50 \times 24 \times 2}{20} = 120 \text{ men}$$

10. Ratio of times taken by Savita and Tripti

$= 125 : 100 = 5 : 4$

Suppose Tripti takes x days to do the work

$$5 : 4 :: 20 : x \Rightarrow \dfrac{5}{4} = \dfrac{20}{x}$$

$$\Rightarrow x = \dfrac{4 \times 20}{5} = 16 \text{ days}$$

Hence, Tripti takes 16 days to complete the work.

11. Sum of the ratios $= 9 + 5 + 4 = 18$

A's share $= \dfrac{9}{18} \times 450 = ₹\ 225.$

12. A can do a work in 16 days

B can do same work in 8 days

A's one day work $= \dfrac{1}{16}$

B's one day work $= \dfrac{1}{8}$

(A + B)'s one day work $= \dfrac{1}{16} + \dfrac{1}{8}$

$$= \dfrac{1+2}{16} = \dfrac{3}{16}$$

(A + B)'s do $\dfrac{3}{16}$ work in 1 day

(A + B)'s do one work in

$$\dfrac{16}{3} = 5\dfrac{1}{3} \text{ days.}$$

13. (A + B)'s 1 day work $= \dfrac{1}{28}$

(A + B + C)'s 1 day work $= \dfrac{1}{21}$

$\therefore$ C's 1 day work $= \dfrac{1}{21} - \dfrac{1}{28}$

$$= \dfrac{4-3}{84} = \dfrac{1}{84}$$

$\therefore$ C can do the work in 84 days.

14. Sapna's 1 day work $= \dfrac{1}{12}$

Sandhya's 1 day work $= \dfrac{1}{10}$

(Sapna + Sandhya)'s 1 day work

$$= \dfrac{1}{12} + \dfrac{1}{10} = \dfrac{5+6}{60} = \dfrac{11}{60}$$

$\because$ They work on alternative days

$\therefore$ (Sapna + Sandhya)'s $5 - 5$ day's work

$$= \dfrac{11}{60} \times 5 = \dfrac{11}{12}$$

$\therefore$ Remaining work $= 1 - \dfrac{11}{12}$

$$= \dfrac{1}{12}$$

Now Sapna's turn comes

Sapna does $\dfrac{1}{12}$ work in 1 day

$\therefore$ Work will be completed in $5 + 5 + 1 = 11$ days

15. Let A alone complete the work in x days

∴ B can complete the work in $2x$ days

A's 1 day work $= \dfrac{1}{x}$

B's 1 day work $= \dfrac{1}{2x}$

C's 1 day work $= \dfrac{1}{x} + \dfrac{1}{2x} = \dfrac{3}{2x}$

(A + B + C)'s 1 day work

$$= \dfrac{1}{x} + \dfrac{1}{2x} + \dfrac{3}{2x} = \dfrac{6}{2x} = \dfrac{3}{x}$$

According to problem,

(A + B + C)'s 1 day work $= \dfrac{1}{7}$

$$\therefore \ \dfrac{3}{x} = \dfrac{1}{7} \ \Rightarrow \ x = 21$$

Hence A alone can do the work in 21 days.

16. Working 7 hours a day 24 men can do a work in 27 days

Working 1 hour a day 1 man can do same work in $27 \times 7 \times 24$ days

Working 9 hours a day 14 men will complete the same work in

$$\dfrac{27 \times 7 \times 24}{9 \times 14} = 36 \text{ days.}$$

17. Work done by (A + B) $= \dfrac{19}{23}$

Work done by (B + C) $= \dfrac{8}{23}$

Work done by (A + B) + (B + C)

$$= \dfrac{19}{23} + \dfrac{8}{23} = \dfrac{27}{23}$$

$\Rightarrow$ A + 2B + C $= \dfrac{27}{23}$

But work done by (A + B + C) = 1 work

Work done by B $= \dfrac{27}{23} - 1 = \dfrac{4}{23}$

Work done by A $= \dfrac{19}{23} - \dfrac{4}{23} = \dfrac{15}{23}$

Work done by C $= \dfrac{8}{23} - \dfrac{4}{23} = \dfrac{4}{23}$

∴ Share of B $= \dfrac{4}{23} \times 529 = ₹ \ 92$

Share of A $= \dfrac{15}{23} \times 529 = ₹ \ 345$

Share of C $= \dfrac{4}{23} \times ₹ \ 529 = ₹ \ 92$

∴ A, B and C should get ₹ 345, ₹ 92, ₹ 92 respectively.

18. Wages of the first man for 3 days
= Work done by him in 3 days
× ₹ 1400

$$= \dfrac{3}{7} \times 1400 = ₹ \ 600$$

Wages of the second man for 3 days
= Work done by him in 3 days
× ₹ 1400

$$= \dfrac{3}{8} \times 1400 = ₹ \ 525$$

∴ Wages of the boy for 3 days
= ₹ 1400 − ₹ (600 + 525)
= ₹ (1400 − 1125) = ₹ 275

Hence their shares will be ₹ 600, ₹ 525 and ₹ 275 respectively.

19. Work done by (3 men + 5 women)

in 1 day $= \dfrac{1}{8}$

or Work done by (24 men + 40 women) in 1 day = 1

Work done by (2 men + 7 boys) in 1 day = $\dfrac{1}{12}$

or Work done by (24 men + 84 boys) in 1 day = 1

24 men + 40 women = 24 men + 84 boys

$\Rightarrow$ 40 women = 84 boys

10 women = 21 boys

$\therefore$ 10 women will work equal to the work done by 21 boys.

20. Suppose work is finished in x days

A works for 4 days, B works for $(x - 2)$ days and C works for x days

$\because$ work done by A in 4 days + work done by B in $(x - 2)$ days + work done by C in x days = 1 work

$\therefore \dfrac{4}{20} + \dfrac{x-2}{12} + \dfrac{x}{18} = 1$

$\Rightarrow \dfrac{36 + 15x - 30 + 10x}{180} = 1$

$\Rightarrow 25x + 6 = 180$

$\Rightarrow 25x = 174$

$\Rightarrow x = \dfrac{174}{25} = 6\dfrac{24}{25}$ days

Hence, work is finished in $6\dfrac{24}{25}$ days.

12

ALLIGATION OR MIXTURE

1. In what proportion must tea at ₹ 62 per kg be mixed with tea at ₹ 72 per kg in order to obtain the mixture worth ₹ 65 per kg?
   A. 4:6   B. 7:3
   C. 2:3   D. 4:7

2. Find the quantity of rice @ ₹ 10 per kg, which should be mixed with 25 kg of rice @ ₹ 8 per kg, so that on selling the mixture @ ₹ 15 per kg there is 80% profit.
   A. 6 kg   B. 7 kg
   C. 3 kg   D. 5 kg

3. Two vessels A and B contain mixture of milk and water in the ratio 4:1 and 9:11 respectively. They are mixed in the ratio of 3:2. Find the ratio of milk : water in the resulting mixture.
   A. 34:16   B. 33:17
   C. 16:34   D. 17:33

4. Two vessels A and B contain milk and water in the ratio 7:5 and 17:7 respectively. In what ratio mixture from two vessels should be mixed to get a new mixture containing milk and water in the ratio 5:3?
   A. 1:2   B. 2:1
   C. 2:3   D. 3:2

5. A shopkeeper has 100 kg of tea. He sells a part of it at 20% profit and the rest at 5% loss. If his overall profit is 10%, find the quantity for each part.
   A. 20 kg   B. 25 kg
   C. 30 kg   D. 40 kg

6. A merchant has 160 kgs of wheat. He sells a part of it at 10% profit and the rest of 6% loss. If he incurs 4% loss on the whole, find the quantity for each part.
   A. 120 kg   B. 140 kg
   C. 150 kg   D. 160 kg

7. A man bought a certain quantity of sugar for ₹ 8000. He sells one-fourth of it at 20% loss. At what per cent profit should he sell the remainder stock so as to make an overall profit of 20%?
   A. 30%   B. 20%
   C. 35%   D. 40%

8. A person covers a distance of 100 km in 10 hours, partly by walking at 7 km/hr and rest by running at 12 km/hr. Find the distance covered in each part.
   A. 48 km   B. 72 km
   C. 108 km   D. 124 km

9. ₹ 675 was divided among 75 boys and girls. Each boy gets ₹ 20 whereas a girl gets ₹ 5. Find the number of boys and girls.

A. 20, 55   B. 15, 60
C. 25, 50   D. 30, 45

10. A sum of ₹ 70 is divided among 10 children. Each boy gets ₹ 10 whereas a girl gets ₹ 5. If the number of boys is 4, find the number of girls.
A. 6   B. 7
C. 8   D. 9

11. A vessel contains 80 litres of milk, 16 litres of milk was taken out of the vessel and replaced by water. Then 16 litres of mixture was withdrawn and again replaced by water. The operation was repeated for third time. How much milk is now left in the vessel?
A. 96.40 *l*   B. 50.36 *l*
C. 40.96 *l*   D. 32.76 *l*

12. A vessel contains mixture of liquids A and B in the ratio 3 : 2. When 20 litres of the mixture is taken out and replaced by 20 litres of liquid B, the ratio changes to 1 : 4. How many litres of liquid A was there initially present in the vessel?
A. 12 *l*   B. 18 *l*
C. 24 *l*   D. 22 *l*

13. A container of 90 litres with two liquids A and B, 60% of liquid A and 30% of liquid B are taken out of the vessel. This leaves the container 40% empty. Find the initial quantity of both liquids.
A. 50 *l*   B. 54 *l*
C. 57 *l*   D. 60 *l*

14. The cost of type-I rice is ₹ 15 per kg and type-II is ₹ 20 per kg. If both type-I and type-II are mixed in the ratio of 2 : 3, then find the price per kg of the mixed variety.
A. ₹ 19.50   B. ₹ 19
C. ₹ 18.50   D. ₹ 18

15. Tea worth ₹ 126 per kg and ₹ 135 per kg are mixed with a third variety in the ratio 1 : 1 : 2. If the mixture is worth ₹ 153 per kg, the price of the third variety per kg will be:
A. ₹ 180   B. ₹ 175.50
C. ₹ 170   D. ₹ 169.50

16. In what ratio of water be mixed with milk to gain $16\frac{2}{3}\%$ on selling the mixture at cost price?
A. 4 : 3   B. 2 : 3
C. 6 : 1   D. 1 : 6

17. In what ratio must a grocer mix two varieties of tea worth ₹ 60 a kg and ₹ 65 a kg so that by selling the mixture at ₹ 68.20 a kg he may gain 10%?
A. 4 : 5   B. 3 : 5
C. 3 : 4   D. 3 : 2

18. A person has two solutions of sugar with 30% and 50% concentration respectively. In what proportion should he mix two solutions to get 45% concentration in the resulting mixture?
A. 1 : 3   B. 3 : 1
C. 2 : 3   D. 3 : 2

19. 6 litres of milk and water mixture has 75% milk in it. How much milk should be added to the mixture to make it 90% pure?

A. 8 *l*   B. 9 *l*

C. 10 *l*   D. 12 *l*

20. In what ratio must water be added

to spirit to gain 25% by selling it at cost price?

A. 1 : 4   B. 4 : 1

C. 3 : 4   D. 4 : 3

ANSWERS

1	2	3	4	5	6	7	8	9	10
B	D	B	B	D	B	A	B	A	A

11	12	13	14	15	16	17	18	19	20
C	B	D	D	B	D	D	A	B	A

EXPLANATORY ANSWERS

1. 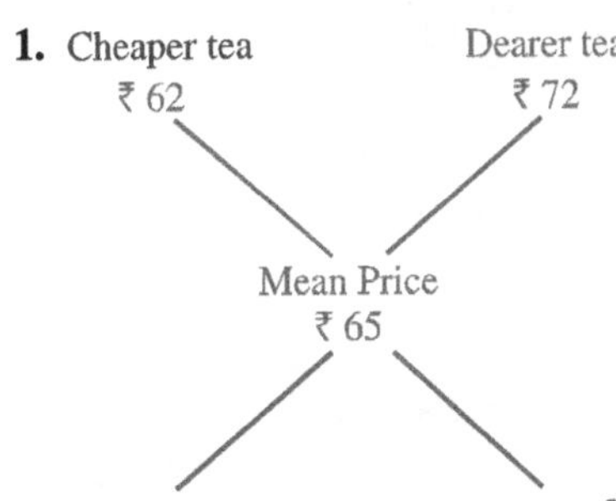

Using Alligation rule,

$$\frac{\text{Quantity of cheaper tea}}{\text{Quantity of dearer tea}} = \frac{d-m}{m-c}$$

$$= \frac{7}{3}$$

Therefore, they must be mixed in the ratio of 7 : 3.

2. 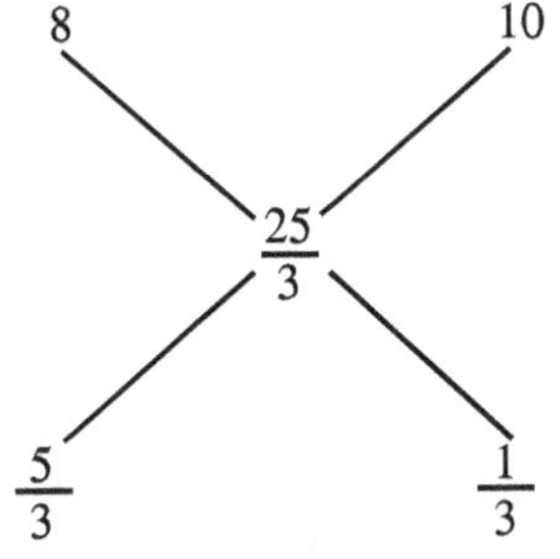

Cost price of the mixture

$$= 15 \times \frac{100}{180} = ₹\ \frac{25}{3} \text{ per kg}$$

$$\frac{\text{Quantity of cheaper rice}}{\text{Quantity of dearer rice}}$$

$$= \frac{5/3}{1/3} = \frac{5}{3} \times \frac{3}{1} = 5 : 1$$

Quantity of dearer rice $= 25 \times \dfrac{1}{5}$

$$= 5 \text{ kg.}$$

3.

Fraction	Milk	Water
A :	$\dfrac{4}{5}$	$\dfrac{1}{5}$
B :	$\dfrac{9}{20}$	$\dfrac{11}{20}$

(3A + 2B) = A and B :

$$\left(\frac{12}{5}+\frac{9}{10}\right) \quad \left(\frac{3}{5}+\frac{22}{20}\right)$$

$$\left(\frac{33}{10}\right) \quad \left(\frac{17}{10}\right)$$

So, Ratio of milk : water in the resulting mixture = 33 : 17.

4. First of all we write the fraction of milk present in three mixture

In A : $\dfrac{7}{12}$

In B : $\dfrac{17}{24}$

In combination of A and B : $\dfrac{5}{8}$

We now apply alligation rule on these fractions.

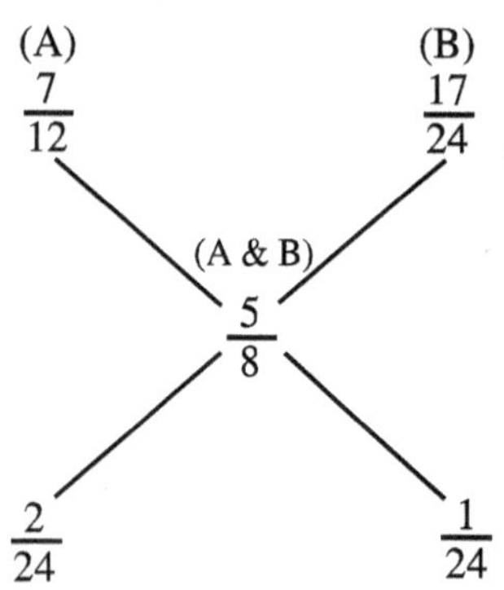

$\therefore$ Ratio of A : B = 2 : 1.

5.

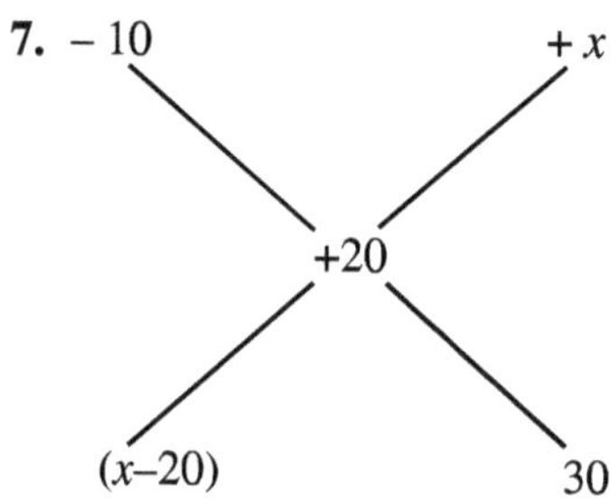

$10 - (-5) = 15$

Ratio $= \dfrac{15}{10} = \dfrac{3}{2} = 3 : 2$

Quantity sold at 20% profit

$= \dfrac{3}{5} \times 100 = 60$ kg

Quantity sold at 5% loss

$= \dfrac{2}{5} \times 100 = 40$ kg

6.

Ratio $= \dfrac{2}{14} = \dfrac{1}{7}$

$= 1 : 7$

Quantity sold at 10% profit

$= \dfrac{1}{8} \times 160$

$= 20$ kg

Quantity sold at 6% loss

$= \dfrac{7}{8} \times 160$

$= 140$ kg.

7.

Let the remainder stock be sold at x% profit.

$$\dfrac{x-20}{30} = \dfrac{1/4}{3/4}$$

$\Rightarrow \qquad x - 20 = 30 \times \dfrac{1}{3} = 10$

$\Rightarrow \qquad x = 10 + 20$

$\qquad\qquad = 30\%$ profit.

8.

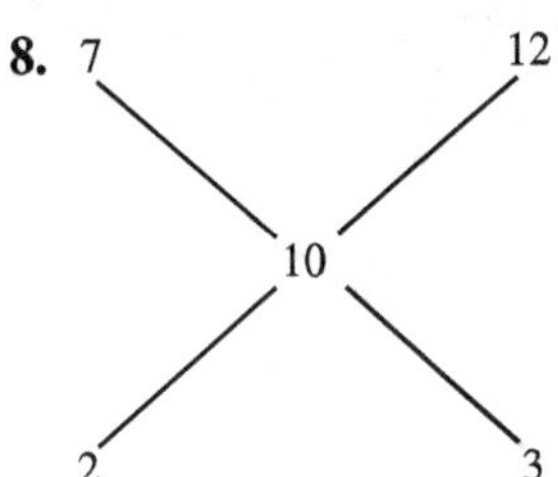

Average speed $= \dfrac{100}{10} = 10$ km/hr.

Ratio of time taken at 7 km/hr to 12 km/hr $= 2 : 3$

Time taken at 7 km/hr

$$= \dfrac{2}{5} \times 10 = 4 \text{ hrs}$$

Distance covered at 7 km/hr

$$= 7 \times 4 = 28 \text{ km}$$

Distance covered at 12 km/hr

$$= 100 - 28 = 72 \text{ km}.$$

9. Average money per head (boy or girl) $= ₹ \dfrac{675}{75} = ₹ 9$

Ratio $= \dfrac{4}{11} = 4 : 11$

Number of boys $= \dfrac{4}{15} \times 75 = 20$

Number of girls $= \dfrac{11}{15} \times 75 = 55.$

10.

$$\dfrac{\text{Number of girls}}{\text{Number of boys}} = \dfrac{3}{2}$$

Number of girls $= \dfrac{3 \times \text{ no. of boys}}{2}$

$$= \dfrac{3 \times 4}{2} = 3 \times 2 = 6.$$

11. Amount of milk left

$$= 80 \left(1 - \dfrac{16}{80}\right)^3 = 80 \left(1 - \dfrac{1}{5}\right)^3$$

$$= 80 \times \dfrac{4}{5} \times \dfrac{4}{5} \times \dfrac{4}{5}$$

$$= \dfrac{80 \times 64}{125} = \dfrac{16 \times 64}{25}$$

$$= \dfrac{1024}{25} = 40.96 \text{ litres.}$$

12. Percentage of liquid B initially present in the vessel

$$= \dfrac{2}{2+3} \times 100 = 40\%$$

Percentage of liquid B finally present in the vessel

$$= \dfrac{4}{1+4} \times 100 = 80\%$$

The second solution is liquid B which is being mixed and it has 100% liquid B.

80% of liquid B present in the resultant mixture may be taken as average percentage. So, using rule of alligation on liquid B per cent, we can write,

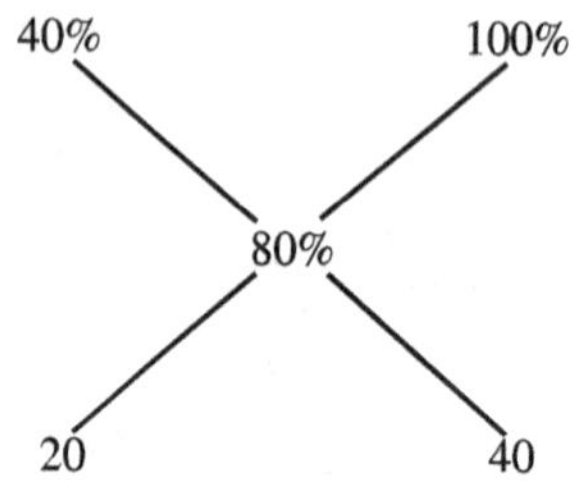

$$\text{Ratio} = \frac{20}{40} = 1 : 2$$

The ratio of liquid left in the vessel to liquid B being mixed = 1 : 2
Since the quantity of liquid B being mixed is 20 litres, the quantity of liquid left in the vessel is 10 litres.

Therefore, the total quantity of liquid initially present in the vessel

$$= 10 + 20 = 30 \text{ litres}$$

Quantity of liquid A

$$= \frac{3}{2+3} \times 30 = 18 \text{ litres.}$$

13. Here withdrawal of liquid A and B result into making the container empty. Hence percentage of two liquids withdrawn are two components of the percentage by which the container becomes empty.

Applying the rule of alligation, we get

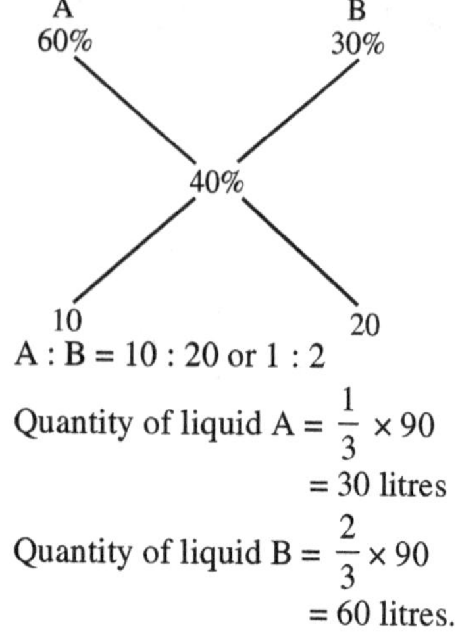

A : B = 10 : 20 or 1 : 2

$$\text{Quantity of liquid A} = \frac{1}{3} \times 90$$
$$= 30 \text{ litres}$$

$$\text{Quantity of liquid B} = \frac{2}{3} \times 90$$
$$= 60 \text{ litres.}$$

14. Let the price per kg of mixed variety be ₹ x; then

By the rule of alligation

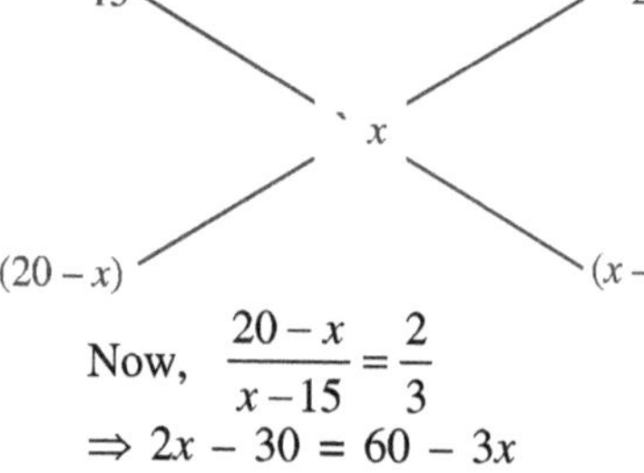

$$\text{Now, } \frac{20 - x}{x - 15} = \frac{2}{3}$$
$$\Rightarrow 2x - 30 = 60 - 3x$$
$$\Rightarrow 5x = 90 \Rightarrow x = ₹ \, 18.$$

15. Here first two varieties of tea are mixed in equal ratio;
So their average price

$$= \frac{126 + 135}{2} = ₹ \, 130.50$$

Let price of the third variety per kg be ₹ x; then now mixture is formed by two varieties one at ₹ 130.50 per kg and other at ₹ x per kg in the same ratio 2 : 2 i.e., 1 : 1.

By the rule of alligation,

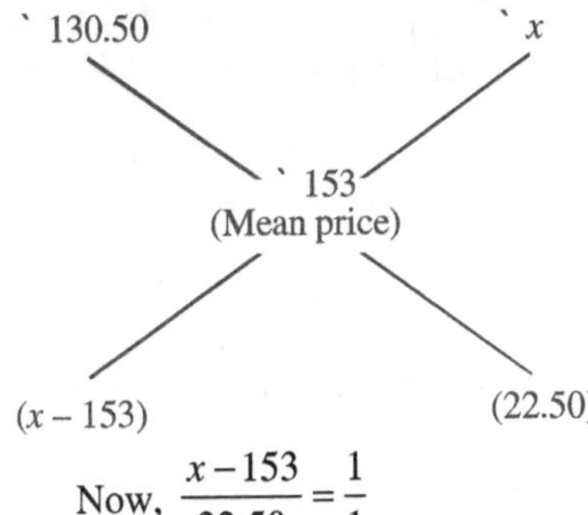

Now, $\dfrac{x-153}{22.50}=\dfrac{1}{1}$

$\Rightarrow \quad x - 153 = 22.50$

$\Rightarrow \qquad x = 153 + 22.50$

$\qquad\qquad = ₹\ 175.50$

16. Let C.P. of 1 litre milk = ₹ 1

gain $= 16\dfrac{2}{3}=\dfrac{50}{3}\%$

and S.P. of 1 litre mixture = ₹ 1
then C.P. of 1 litre mixture

$$= 1\times\dfrac{100\times 3}{350}=₹\ \dfrac{6}{7}$$

By the rule of alligation,

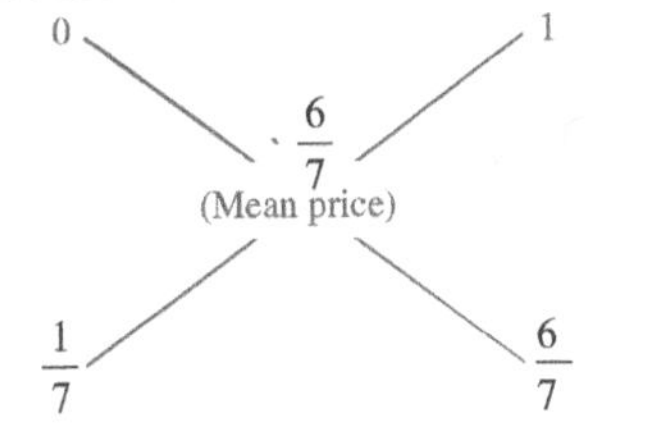

Hence, required ratio

$$= \dfrac{1}{7}:\dfrac{6}{7}=1:6$$

17. S.P. of 1 kg mixture = ₹ 68.20,
gain = 10%
Hence, C.P. of 1 kg mixture

$$= \dfrac{100}{110}\times ₹\ 68.20 = ₹\ 62$$

By the rule of alligation

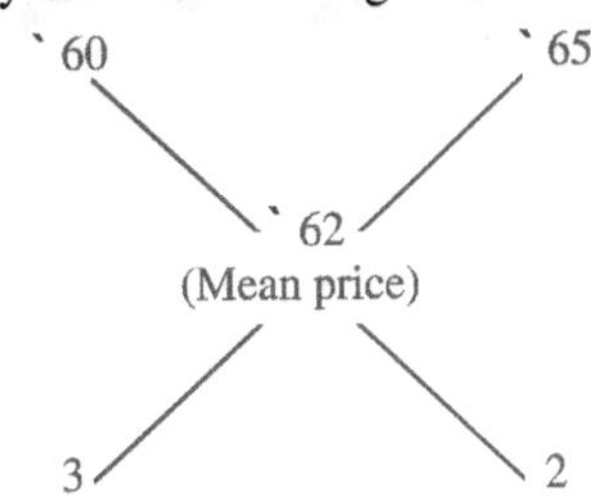

Required ratio = 3 : 2

18. 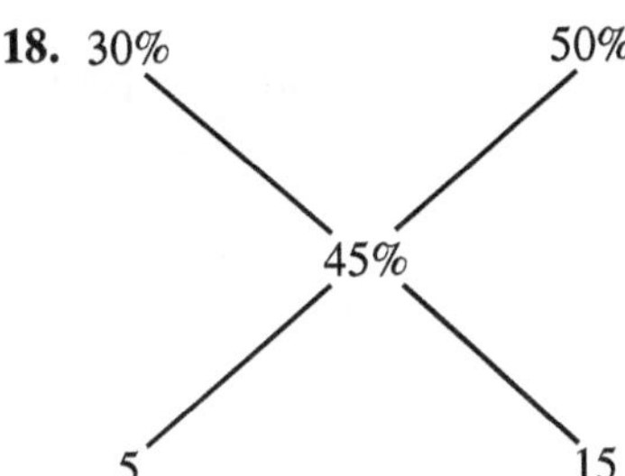

He should mix 30% and 50% in
the ratio 5 : 15 = 1 : 3

$$\dfrac{30\%\ \text{Solution}}{50\%\ \text{Solution}}=\dfrac{1}{3}=1:3.$$

19. The given solution has 75% milk.
Milk to be added has 100% milk.

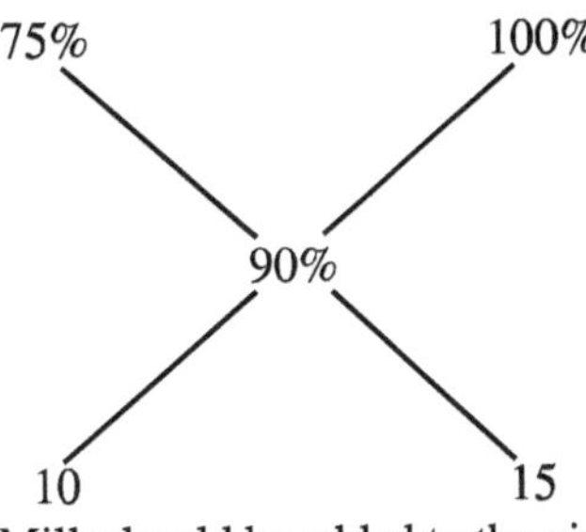

Milk should be added to the given
mixture in the ratio 15 : 10 = 3 : 2

$\therefore$ Quantity of milk to be added

$$= \dfrac{3}{2}\times 6 = 9 \text{ litres.}$$

20. 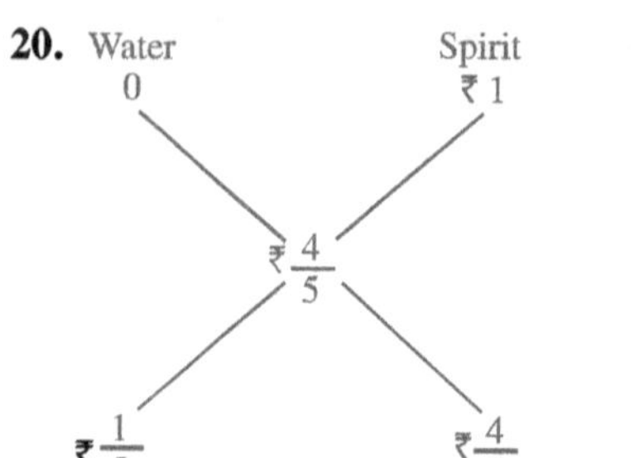

Let cost price of spirit be ₹ 1 per litre.

Then SP of mixture = ₹ 1 per litre

gain = 25%

So, CP of mixture = $1 \times \dfrac{100}{125}$

$$= ₹\ \dfrac{4}{5}$$

We assume that CP of water is zero using alligation rule on cost price, water should be mixed to spirit in the ratio $\dfrac{1}{5} : \dfrac{4}{5}$ or $1 : 4$.

13

AREA AND PERIMETER

1. The width of a rectangular hall is $\frac{3}{4}$ of its length. If the area of the hall is 300 m², then the difference between its length and width is:
   A. 3 m
   B. 4 m
   C. 5 m
   D. 15 m

2. A room 8 m × 6 m is to be carpeted by a carpet 2 m wide. The length of carpet required is :
   A. 12 m
   B. 36 m
   C. 24 m
   D. 48 m

3. The dimensions of the floor of a rectangular hall are 4 m × 3 m. The floor of the hall is to be tiled fully with 8 cm × 6 cm rectangular tiles without breaking tiles to smaller sizes. The number of tiles required is:
   A. 4800
   B. 2600
   C. 2500
   D. 2400

4. The length and breadth of a playground are 36 m and 21 m respectively. Flagstaffs are required to be fixed on all along the boundary at a distance 3 m apart. The number of flagstaffs will be :
   A. 37
   B. 38
   C. 39
   D. 40

5. A rectangular carpet has an area of 120 m² and a perimeter of 46 m. The length of its diagonal is:
   A. 15 m
   B. 16 m
   C. 17 m
   D. 20 m

6. A rectangle is having 15 cm as its length and 150 cm² as its area. Its area is increased to $1\frac{1}{3}$ times the original area by increasing only its length. Its new perimeter is:
   A. 50 cm
   B. 60 cm
   C. 70 cm
   D. 80 cm

7. A man walked 20 m to cross a rectangular field diagonally. If the length of the field is 16 m, the breadth of the field is:
   A. 4 m
   B. 16 m
   C. 12 m
   D. Can not be determined

8. If only the length of a rectangular plot is reduced to $\frac{2}{3}$ rd of its original length, the ratio of original area to reduced area is:
   A. 2 : 3
   B. 3 : 2
   C. 1 : 2
   D. None of these

9. The length and breadth of a square are increased by 40% and 30% respectively. The area of resulting rectangle exceeds the area of the square by :
A. 42%
B. 62%
C. 82%
D. None of these

10. The area of a rectangle is thrice that of a square. Length of the rectangle is 40 cm and breadth of rectangle is $\dfrac{3}{2}$ times that of the side of the square.

The side of the square in cms is:
A. 60   B. 20
C. 30   D. 15

11. If the perimeter of a rhombus is 4 a and lengths of the diagonals are x and y, then its area is:
A. $a(x + y)$ B. $x^2 + y^2$

C. xy D. $\dfrac{1}{2}xy$

12. In a rhombus whose area is 144 cm^2. One of its diagonals is twice as long as the other. The lengths of its diagonals are :
A. 24 cm, 48 cm
B. 12 cm, 24 cm
C. $6\sqrt{2}$ cm, $12\sqrt{2}$ cm
D. 6 cm, 12 cm

13. If each of the dimensions of a rectangle is increased by 100%, its area is increased by
A. 100%   B. 200%
C. 300%   D. 400%

14. The legs of a right triangle are in the ratio of 1 : 2 and its area is 36. The hypotenuse of the triangle is:
A. 3   B. $\sqrt{5}$
C. $\sqrt{3}$ D. $6\sqrt{5}$

15. Each side of an equilateral triangle is increased by 1.5%. The percentage increase in its area is:
A. 1.5%   B. 3%
C. 4.5%   D. 5.7%

16. The circumference of a circle is 352 m. Its area is:
A. 9856 m^2 B. 8956 m^2
C. 6589 m^2 D. 5986 m^2

17. The diameter of a wheel is 2 cm. It rolls forward covering 10 revolutions. The distance travelled by it is:
A. 3.14 cm   B. 62.8 cm
C. 31.4 cm   D. 125.6 cm

18. The length of a minute hand on a wall clock is 7 cm. The area swept by the minute hand in 30 minutes is :
A. 147 cm^2 B. 210 cm^2
C. 154 cm^2 D. 77 cm^2

19. A circular wire of radius 42 cm is cut and bent in the form of a rectangle whose sides are in ratio 6 : 5. The smaller side of the rectangle is :
A. 30 cm   B. 60 cm
C. 72 cm   D. 132 cm

20. The perimeter of a semi-circle of 56 cm diameter will be :
A. 144 cm   B. 232 cm
C. 154 cm   D. 116 cm

ANSWERS

1	2	3	4	5	6	7	8	9	10
C	C	C	B	C	B	C	B	C	B

11	12	13	14	15	16	17	18	19	20
D	B	C	D	A	A	B	D	B	A

EXPLANATORY ANSWERS

1. Let length of rectangular hall
$$= x \text{ m.}$$
$\therefore$ breadth of rectangular hall
$$= \frac{3}{4}x \text{ m}$$
Area of rectangular hall
$$= l \times b = x \times \frac{3x}{4} = \frac{3x^2}{4} \text{ m}^2$$
But area of rectangular hall
$$= 300 \text{ m}^2$$
$$\therefore \quad \frac{3x^2}{4} = 300$$
$$\Rightarrow x^2 = \frac{4 \times 300}{3} = 400$$
$$\Rightarrow x = 20$$
$\therefore$ length = 20 m and breadth
$$= \frac{3}{4} \times 20 = 15 \text{ m}$$
Difference = 20 – 15 = 5 m.

2. Area of room = 8 × 6 = 48m^2

$$\text{Length of carpet} = \frac{\text{Area}}{\text{breadth}} = \frac{48}{2}$$
$$= 24 \text{ m.}$$

3. Length of hall = 4 m = 4 × 100
$$= 400 \text{ cm}$$
breadth of hall = 3 m = 3 × 100
$$= 300 \text{ cm}$$
Area of the floor = $l \times b$

$$= 400 \times 300 \text{ cm}^2$$
Area of the tile = 8 × 6 = 48 cm^2

$$\text{Number to tiles} = \frac{400 \times 300}{48}$$
$$= 2500.$$

4.

A D ________ C, 21 m, 36 m

length of play ground = 36 m
breadth of play ground = 21 m
perimeter of playground = $2(l + b)$
$$= 2(36 + 21) = 2 \times 57 = 114 \text{ m}$$

$$\text{Number of flagstaffs} = \frac{114}{3} = 38.$$

5. Perimeter of rectangle = $2(l + b)$
According to the question,
$$2(l + b) = 46$$
$$\therefore \quad l + b = 23 \qquad \text{...}(i)$$
Area of rectangle = $l \times b$
$$l \times b = 120 \qquad \text{...}(ii)$$
Now $(l - b)^2 = (l + b)^2 - 4lb$
$$[\because (a - b)^2 = (a + b)^2 - 4ab]$$
$$= (23)^2 - 4 \times 120$$
$$= 529 - 480 = 49$$
$$\therefore \quad l - b = 7 \qquad \text{...}(iii)$$
Solving (iii) and (i) we get
$$l = 15 \text{ and } b = 8$$

$\therefore$ Diagonal of rectangle

$$= \sqrt{l^2 + b^2} = \sqrt{(15)^2 + (8)^2}$$

$$= \sqrt{225 + 64} = \sqrt{289}$$

$$= 17 \text{ m.}$$

6. Area of rectangle = 150 cm^2
length of rectangle = 15 cm

$$\therefore \text{ breadth of rectangle} = \frac{150}{15}$$

$$= 10 \text{ cm}$$

$$\text{New area} = \left(150 \times \frac{4}{3}\right) = 200 \text{ cm}^2$$

$$\therefore \text{ New length} = \frac{\text{New area}}{\text{Original breadth}}$$

$$\frac{200}{10} = 20 \text{ cm}$$

New perimeter = 2(20 + 10)

$$= 60 \text{ cm.}$$

7.

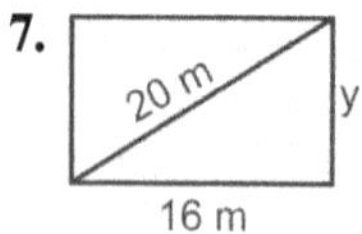

Breadth of rectangle

$$= \sqrt{(20)^2 - (16)^2}$$

$$= \sqrt{400 - 256}$$

$$= \sqrt{144} = 12 \text{ m.}$$

8. Let length = x and breadth = y

New length = $\dfrac{2}{3}x$ and breadth = y

$$\therefore \frac{\text{Original area}}{\text{Reduced area}} = \frac{xy}{\frac{2}{3}xy} = \frac{3}{2}$$

$$= 3 : 2.$$

9. Let original side = x
Area = x^2

New area = $\left(\dfrac{140}{100}x \times \dfrac{130}{100}x\right)$

$$= \frac{91}{50}x^2$$

Change in area = $\left(\dfrac{91}{50}x^2 - x^2\right)$

$$= \frac{91x^2 - 50x^2}{50}$$

$$= \frac{41x^2}{50}$$

Increase percent

$$= \frac{41x^2}{50} \times \frac{1}{x^2} \times 100 = 80\%.$$

10. Length of rectangle = 40 cm
Let side of square = x cm

Breadth of rectangle = $\dfrac{3}{2}x$ cm

$$40 \times \frac{3}{2}x = 3x^2$$

$$\Rightarrow x = 20$$

Hence, side of square = 20 cm.

11. Area of rhombus = $\dfrac{1}{2} \times d_1 \times d_2$

$$= \frac{1}{2}xy.$$

12. Let diagonals of rhombus are x cm and $2x$ cm

Area of rhombus = $\dfrac{1}{2} \times d_1 \times d_2$

$$\Rightarrow \quad \frac{1}{2} \times x \times 2x = 144$$

$$\Rightarrow \quad x^2 = 144$$

$$\Rightarrow \quad x = 12$$

$\therefore$ Diagonals are 12 cm and 24 cm.

13. Let length $= x$ and breadth $= y$

then, Area $= xy$

New length $= 2x$

and new breadth $= 2y$

Area $= 2x \times 2y = 4xy$

$\therefore$ Increase percent $= \dfrac{3xy}{xy} \times 100$

$= 300\%.$

14. $\dfrac{1}{2} \times x \times 2x = 36 \Rightarrow x^2 = 36$

$\Rightarrow \qquad x = 6$

$\therefore$ Hypotenuse $= \sqrt{6^2 + 12^2}$

$= \sqrt{36 + 144}$

$= \sqrt{180}$

$= 6\sqrt{5}.$

15. Let original length of each side $= a$

Then, area $= \dfrac{\sqrt{3}}{4} a^2 = A$

New area $= \dfrac{\sqrt{3}}{4}\left[\left(\dfrac{101.5}{100} a\right)^2\right]$

$= \dfrac{\sqrt{3}}{4}\left(\dfrac{20.3}{20}\right) a^2 = \left(\dfrac{20.3}{20}\right) A$

Increase in area

$= \left(\dfrac{0.3}{20} A \times \dfrac{1}{A} \times 100\right) = 1.5\%.$

16. $2\pi r = 352$

$\Rightarrow 2 \times \dfrac{22}{7} \times r = 352$

$\Rightarrow r = \dfrac{7 \times 352}{2 \times 22} = 56$ m

Area $= \pi r^2 = \dfrac{22}{7} \times 56 \times 56$

$= 22 \times 8 \times 56 = 9856$ m^2.

17. Distance covered in 1 revolution

$= 2\pi(1) = 2 \times \dfrac{22}{7} \times 1 = \dfrac{44}{7}$ cm

Distance covered in 10 revolutions

$= \dfrac{44}{7} \times 10 = \dfrac{440}{7} = 62.8$ cm.

18. Angle formed in 30 minute

$= \dfrac{360}{60} \times 30 = 180°$

Area swept by min. hand

$= \dfrac{\theta}{360} \times \pi r^2$

$= \dfrac{180}{360} \times \dfrac{22}{7} \times 7 \times 7 = 77$ cm^2

19. Let length $= 6x$ and breadth $= 5x$

$2(l + b) = 2\pi r$

$l + b = \pi r$

$6x + 5x = \dfrac{22}{7} \times 42$

$\Rightarrow \qquad 11x = 22 \times 6 = 132$

$\Rightarrow \qquad x = \dfrac{132}{11} = 12$

$6x = 12 \times 6 = 72$ cm

$5x = 12 \times 5 = 60$ cm

$\therefore$ Smaller side $= 60$ cm.

20.

Diameter of semi-circle $= 56$ cm

$\therefore$ radius of semi-circle $= 28$ cm

Perimeter of semicircle

$=$ Circumference of semicircle

$+$ diameter

$= \pi r + 2r$

$= \dfrac{22}{7} \times 28 + 56$

$= 22 \times 4 + 56$

$= 88 + 56 = 144$ cm

14

VOLUME AND SURFACE AREA

1. If the length, breadth and height of a cuboid are 2 m, 2 m and 1 m respectively, then its surface area (in m^2) is :
   A. 8
   B. 12
   C. 16
   D. 24

2. The length of a longest rod that can be placed in a room 30 m long, 24 m broad and 18 m high is:

   A. 30 m
   B. $15\sqrt{2}$ m
   C. 60 m
   D. $30\sqrt{2}$ m

3. The surface area of a cube is 1176 cm^2. The volume of this cube is:
   A. 7056 cm^3
   B. 4704 cm^3
   C. 2744 cm^3
   D. 3528 cm^3

4. The volume of a cube is 125 cm^3. The surface area of the cube is :
   A. 625 cm^2
   B. 125 cm^2
   C. 150 cm^2
   D. 100 cm^2

5. The length of a cylinder is 80 cm and the diameter of its base is 7 cm. The whole surface of the cylinder is:
   A. 1837 cm^2
   B. 1760 cm^2
   C. 3080 cm^2
   D. 1942 cm^2

6. The radii of two cylinders are in the ratio of 2 : 3 and their heights are in the ratio 5 : 3. The ratio of their volumes is:
   A. 27 : 20
   B. 20 : 27
   C. 4 : 9
   D. 9 : 4

7. The radius of base of a right circular cone is 6 cm and its slant height is 28 cm. The curved surface of the cone is:
   A. 268 cm^2
   B. 658 cm^2
   C. 462 cm^2
   D. 528 cm^2

8. If a right circular cone of verticle height 24 cm has a volume of 1232 cm^3, then the area of its curved surface in cm^2 is:
   A. 1254
   B. 704
   C. 550
   D. 154

9. If the volumes of two cones are in the ratio 1 : 4 and their diameters are in ratio 4 : 5, then the ratio of their heights is :
   A. 1 : 5
   B. 5 : 4
   C. 5 : 16
   D. 25 : 64

10. A reservoir is in the shape of a frustum of a right circular cone. It is 8 m across at the top and 4 m across the bottom. It is 6m deep. Its capacity is:
    A. 176 m^3
    B. 196 m^3
    C. 200 m^3
    D. 110 m^3

11. A cylindrical piece of metal of radius 2 cm and height 6 cm is shaped in to a cone of same radius. The height of cone is:

A. 18 cm   B. 14 cm
C. 12 cm   D. 8 cm

12. The curved surface area of a sphere is 1386 cm^2. Its volume is:
A. 2772 cm^3 B. 4158 cm^3
C. 4851 cm^3 D. 5544 cm^3

13. Six spherical balls of radius r are melted and cast into a cylindrical rod of metal of same radius. The height of rod will be:
A. 4 r B. 6 r
C. 8 r D. 12 r

14. The number of solid spheres, each of diameter 6 cm, that could be moulded to form a solid metal cylinder of height 45 cm and diameter 4 cm, is :
A. 3   B. 4
C. 5   D. 6

15. If the volume and surface area of a sphere are numerically the same, then its radius is :
A. 1 unit   B. 2 units
C. 3 units   D. 4 units

16. If each side of a cube is doubled, then its volume:
A. is doubled

B. becomes 4 times
C. becomes 6 times
D. becomes 8 times

17. The radius of a wire is decrease to one third. If volume remains same, length will increase:
A. 1 time   B. 6 times
C. 3 times   D. 9 times

18. Three cubes whose edges are 3 cm, 4 cm and 5 cm respectively are melted without any loss of metal into a single cube. The edge of new cube is:
A. 12 cm   B. 10 cm
C. 9 cm   D. 6 cm

19. A metal sheet 27 cm long, 8 cm broad and 1 cm thick is melted in to a cube. The difference between the surface areas of two solids will be:
A. 284 cm^2 B. 296 cm^2
C. 286 cm^2 D. 300 cm^2

20. Find the length of the longest pole that can be put in a room 12 m long, 8 m broad and 9 m height.
A. 12 m   B. 13 m
C. 17 m   D. 23 m

ANSWERS

1	2	3	4	5	6	7	8	9	10
C	D	C	C	A	B	D	C	D	A

11	12	13	14	15	16	17	18	19	20
A	C	C	C	C	D	D	D	C	C

EXPLANATORY ANSWERS

1. Surface area of cuboid
$$= 2(lb + bh + hl)$$
$$= 2(2 \times 2 + 2 \times 1 + 2 \times 1)$$
$$= 2(4 + 2 + 2)$$
$$= 2 \times 8$$
$$= 16 \text{ m}^2.$$

2. Length of the longest rod

$$= \sqrt{l^2 + b^2 + h^2}$$

$$= \sqrt{30^2 + 24^2 + 18^2}$$

$$= \sqrt{900 + 576 + 324}$$

$$= \sqrt{1800} = \sqrt{900 \times 2}$$

$$= 30\sqrt{2} \text{ m.}$$

3. Surface area of cube $= 6a^2$

$$\Rightarrow 6a^2 = 1176$$

$$\Rightarrow a^2 = \frac{1176}{6} = 196$$

$$\Rightarrow a = 14$$

Volume of cube $= (a)^3$

$$= 14 \times 14 \times 14 = 4744 \text{ m}^3.$$

4. Volume of cube $= a^3 \Rightarrow a^3 = 125$

$$\Rightarrow \qquad a = 5$$

$\therefore$ Side of cube $= 5$ cm

Surface area of cube $= 6a^2$

$$= 6 \times 5 \times 5 = 150 \text{ cm}^2.$$

5. Total surface area of cylinder

$$= 2\pi r(h + r)$$

$$= 2 \times \frac{22}{7} \times \frac{7}{2} \left(80 + \frac{7}{2} \right)$$

$$= 22 \left(\frac{167}{2} \right) = 11 \times 167$$

$$= 1837 \text{ cm}^2.$$

6. Let radii of the cylinders be $2r$ and $3r$ and their heights be $5h$ and $3h$ respectively.

$$\text{Required ratio} = \frac{\pi(2r)^2 \times 5h}{\pi(3r)^2 \times 3h}$$

$$= \frac{4r^2 \times 5h}{9r^2 \times 3h} = \frac{20}{27} = 20 : 27.$$

7. Curved surface area of cone $= \pi rl$

$$= \frac{22}{7} \times 6 \times 28$$

$$= 22 \times 24 = 528 \text{ cm}^2.$$

8. Volume of cone $= \frac{1}{3}\pi r^2 h$

$$\Rightarrow \frac{1}{3} \times \frac{22}{7} \times r^2 \times 24 = 1232$$

$$\Rightarrow r^2 = \frac{3 \times 7 \times 1232}{22 \times 24} = 7 \times 7$$

$$\Rightarrow r = 7$$

Slant height $= \sqrt{24^2 + 7^2}$

$$= \sqrt{576 + 49}$$

$$= \sqrt{625} = 25 \text{ cm}$$

$\therefore$ Curved surface area of cone

$$= \pi rl$$

$$= \frac{22}{7} \times 7 \times 25$$

$$= 550 \text{ cm}^2.$$

9. Let the diameters of bases of the cones be $4r$ and $5r$ and their heights be h and H respectively.

$$\text{Then, } \frac{\frac{1}{3}\pi \left(\frac{4r}{2} \right)^2 \times h}{\frac{1}{3}\pi \left(\frac{5r}{2} \right)^2 \times H} = \frac{1}{4}$$

$$\Rightarrow \frac{16\,h}{25\,H} = \frac{1}{4}$$

$$\Rightarrow 64\,h = 25\,H$$

$$\Rightarrow \frac{h}{H} = \frac{25}{64}$$

$$\therefore \quad h : H = 25 : 64$$

10. Volume of frustum

$$= \frac{1}{3}\pi h(R^2 + r^2 + Rr)$$

where R = 4 m, r = 2 m, h = 6m

$$= \frac{1}{3} \times \frac{22}{7} \times 6(16 + 4 + 8) \, m^3$$

$$= \frac{22}{7} \times 2 \times 28$$

$$= 22 \times 8 = 176 \, m^3.$$

11. Volume of cone = Volume of cylinder

$$\Rightarrow \frac{1}{3}\pi r^2 h = \pi r^2 \times 6$$

$$\Rightarrow \frac{1}{3} \times (2)^2 \times h = (2)^2 \times 6$$

$$\Rightarrow \frac{h}{3} = 6 \Rightarrow h = 18 \, cm$$

Hence, height of cone = 18 cm.

12. Curved surface area of sphere $= 4\pi r^2$

$$\Rightarrow 4 \times \frac{22}{7} \times r^2 = 1386$$

$$\Rightarrow r^2 = \frac{7 \times 1386}{4 \times 22} = \frac{7 \times 63}{4}$$

$$= \frac{7 \times 7 \times 9}{4}$$

$$\Rightarrow r = \frac{7 \times 3}{2} = \frac{21}{2}$$

Volume of sphere $= \frac{4}{3}\pi r^3$

$$= \frac{4}{3} \times \frac{22}{7} \times \frac{21}{2} \times \frac{21}{2} \times \frac{21}{2}$$

$$= 441 \times 11 = 4851 \, cm^3.$$

13. According to the question

$$6 \times \frac{4}{3}\pi r^3 = \pi r^2 h$$

$$8r = h$$

$$\Rightarrow \quad h = 8r.$$

14. $n \times \dfrac{4}{3}\pi(3)^3 = \pi \times (2)^2 \times 45$

$$\Rightarrow n \times \frac{4}{3} \times 27 = 4 \times 45$$

$$\Rightarrow 9n = 45 \Rightarrow n = \frac{45}{9} = 5$$

Hence number of spheres = 5

15. Let radius of sphere = r units

Volume of sphere = Surface area of sphere

$$\Rightarrow \frac{4}{3}\pi r^3 = 4\pi r^2$$

$$\Rightarrow \frac{r^3}{r^2} = 3 \Rightarrow r = 3 \text{ units.}$$

16. Let each side of cube = x

Volume = $(x)^3$

Now each side of cube = $2x$

Volume = $(2x)^3 = 8x^3$

Hence, each side of cube is doubled then its volume becomes 8 times.

17. Let radius = R and length = h

Volume = $\pi R^2 h$

New radius = $\dfrac{1}{3}$R,

Let new length = H

Volume = $\pi\left(\dfrac{1}{3}R\right)^2 \times H = \dfrac{\pi R^2 H}{9}$

According to the question,

$$\pi R^2 h = \frac{\pi R^2 H}{9}$$

$$\Rightarrow \quad H = 9h.$$

18.
$$V_1 = (3)^3 = 27 \text{ cm}^3$$
$$V_2 = (4)^3 = 64 \text{ cm}^3$$
$$V_3 = (5)^3 = 125 \text{ cm}^3$$
$$V_1 + V_2 + V_3 = 27 + 64 + 125$$
$$= 216 \text{ cm}^3$$
$$V = 216 \text{ cm}^3$$

$$\Rightarrow \text{Side of new cube} = \sqrt[3]{216}$$
$$= 6 \text{ cm}.$$

19. Volume of new cube formed
$$= 27 \times 8 \times 1 = 216 \text{ cm}^3$$

Edge of this cube $= \sqrt[3]{216}$
$$= 6 \text{ cm}$$
Surface area of this cube $= 6a^2$
$$= 6 \times (6)^2 = 6 \times 36 = 216 \text{ cm}^2$$

Surface area of given cuboid
$$= 2(lb + bh + hl)$$
$$= 2(27 \times 8 + 8 \times 1 + 1 \times 27)$$
$$= 2(216 + 8 + 27)$$
$$= 2(251) = 502 \text{ cm}^2$$

$\therefore$ Difference between the surface areas
$$= 502 - 216 = 286 \text{ cm}^2.$$

20. Length of the longest pole
$$= \sqrt{l^2 + b^2 + h^2}$$
$$= \sqrt{(12)^2 + (8)^2 + (9)^2}$$
$$= \sqrt{144 + 64 + 81}$$
$$= \sqrt{289} = 17 \text{ m}.$$

15

PIPES AND CISTERNS

1. Two pipes P and Q can fill a cistern in 12 and 15 minutes respectively. Both are opened together, but at the end of three minutes the first is turned off. How much longer will the cistern take to fill?

   A. $8\frac{1}{4}$ min.
   B. $11\frac{1}{4}$ min.
   C. $7\frac{1}{4}$ min.
   D. $15\frac{1}{4}$ min.

2. A tap can fill a tank in 12 hours, where as another can empty it in 18 hours. If both the taps are opened. Simultaneously, how much time will the tank take to fill?

   A. 36 hrs.
   B. 72 hrs.
   C. 18 hrs.
   D. 12 hrs.

3. 12 pumps working 6 hours a day empty a completely filled reservoir in 15 days. How many such pumps working 9 hrs a day will empty the same reservoir in 12 days?

   A. 9
   B. 10
   C. 12
   D. 15

4. A tank is filled in 5 hours by three pipes A, B and C. The pipe C is twice as fast as B and B is twice as fast as A. How much time will pipe A alone take to fill the tank?

   A. 40 hrs.
   B. 35 hrs.
   C. 30 hrs.
   D. 25 hrs.

5. Two pipes A and B together can fill a tank is 4 hrs. Had they been opened separately, then B would have taken 6 hrs. more than A to fill the tank separately?

   A. 8 hrs.
   B. 6 hrs.
   C. 2 hrs.
   D. 1 hr.

6. A tap can fill a cistern in 8 hrs and another can empty it in 16 hrs. If both the taps are opened, the time (in hrs) to fill the tank is:

   A. 8
   B. 10
   C. 16
   D. 24

7. A cystern can be filled by pipes A and B in 20 hrs and 30 hrs respectively. When full, the tank can be emptied by pipe C in 40 hrs. If all the taps be turned on at the same time, the cystern will be full in:

   A. 10 hrs.
   B. 90 hrs.
   C. 16 hrs.
   D. $17\frac{1}{7}$ hrs.

8. A cystern is normally filled in 8 hrs but takes 2 hrs longer to fill because of a leak in its bottom. If

the cystern is full, the leak will empty it in:

A. 16 hrs.   B. 40 hrs.
C. 25 hrs.   D. 20 hrs.

9. Pipes A and B can fill a tank in 20 minutes and 25 minutes respectively. If both the taps are opened and after 5 minutes, pipe B is turned off, the tank will be completely filled in:

A. $17\frac{1}{2}$ min.   B. 12 min.

C. 11 min.   D. 6 min.

10. A tap can fill a tank in 16 minutes and another can empty it in 8 minutes. If the tank is already half full and both the tanks are opened together, the tank will be:
A. filled in 12 min.
B. emptied in 12 min.
C. filled in 8 min.
D. emptied in 8 min.

11. Two taps can separately fill a cistern in 10 min. and 15 min. respectively and when the waste pipe is opened they can together fill it in 18 minutes. The waste pipe can empty the full cistern in:
A. 6 min.   B. 9 min.
C. 13 min.   D. 23 min.

12. Two pipes can fill a tank in 10 hrs. and 15 hrs. respectively. Both together can fill it in:

A. $12\frac{1}{2}$ hrs

B. 5 hrs
C. 6 hrs
D. None of these

13. Two pipes A and B would fill a cistern in 20 and 34 minutes respectively. Both pipes being opened, find when the first pipe must be turned off so that the cistern may be just filled in 17 minutes?
A. 10 min.   B. 30 min.
C. 17 min.   D. 34 min.

14. Pipe A and B can fill a tank in 10 hrs and 15 hrs respectively. Both together can fill it in:
A. 6 hrs   B. 7 hrs
C. 8 hrs   D. 9 hrs

15. A cistern is normally filled in 8 hrs but takes two hours longer to fill because of a leak in its bottom. If the cistern is full, the leak will empty it in:
A. 20 hrs   B. 30 hrs
C. 40 hrs   D. 50 hrs

16. One pipe can fill a tank three times as fast as another pipe. If together the two pipes can fill the tank in 36 minutes, then the slower pipe alone will be able to fill the tank in:
A. 192 min   B. 144 min
C. 108 min   D. 81 min

17. A large tanker can be filled by two pipes A and B in 60 minutes and 40 minutes respectively. How many minutes will it take to fill the tanker from empty state if B is used for half the time and A and B fill it together for the other half?
A. 30 min   B. 27.5 min
C. 20 min   D. 15 min

18. Two pipes A and B can fill a cistern in $37\dfrac{1}{2}$ min and 45 min respectively. Both pipes are opened. The cistern will be filled in just half an hour, if pipe B is turned off after:

A. 15 min   B. 10 min
C. 9 min   D. 5 min

19. Two pipes A and B can fill a tank in 24 min and 32 min respectively. If both the pipes are opened simultaneously, after how much time B should be close so that the tank is full in 18 minutes?

A. 6 min   B. 8 min
C. 10 min   D. 12 min

20. A water tank is two-fifth full. Pipe A can fill a tank in 10 minutes and pipe B can empty it in 6 minutes. If both the pipes are opened, how long will it take to empty or fill the tank completely?

A. 6 min to fill
B. 6 min to empty
C. 9 min to fill
D. 9 min to empty

ANSWERS

1	2	3	4	5	6	7	8	9	10
A	A	B	B	B	C	D	B	C	D

11	12	13	14	15	16	17	18	19	20
B	C	A	A	C	B	A	C	B	B

EXPLANATORY ANSWERS

1. In 3 minutes the part filled by both pipes P and Q

$$= 3 \times \left(\frac{1}{12} + \frac{1}{15}\right) = 3\left(\frac{5+4}{60}\right)$$

$$= 3 \times \frac{9}{60} = \frac{9}{20}$$

Remaining part $= 1 - \dfrac{9}{20} = \dfrac{11}{20}$

Time taken by pipe Q to fill the remaining part

$$= \frac{11/20}{1/15} = \frac{11}{20} \times \frac{15}{1}$$

$$= \frac{33}{4} = 8\frac{1}{4} \text{ min.}$$

2. In 1 hour the part filled by both the taps

$$= \frac{1}{12} - \frac{1}{18} = \frac{3-2}{36} = \frac{1}{36}$$

Hence, both the taps can fill the tank in 36 hrs.

3. In one day working 1 hour a day the filled reservoir can be emptied by $12 \times 6 \times 15$ pumps.

Hence, in 12 days working 9 hours a day the filled reservoir

can be emptied by $\dfrac{12 \times 6 \times 15}{12 \times 9}$

$= 10$ pumps.

4. Let x, $\dfrac{x}{2}$ and $\dfrac{x}{4}$ hours be the time taken by pipes A, B and C respectively to fill the tank, then

$$\frac{1}{x} + \frac{2}{x} + \frac{4}{x} = \frac{1}{5}$$

$$\Rightarrow \frac{7}{x} = \frac{1}{5} \Rightarrow x = 35$$

Hence, time taken by A is 35 hrs. to fill the tank.

5. Let x and $(x+6)$ hours be the time taken by pipes A and B respectively to fill the cistern, then,

$$\frac{1}{x} + \frac{1}{x+6} = \frac{1}{4}$$

$$\Rightarrow \frac{x+6+x}{x(x+6)} = \frac{1}{4}$$

$$\Rightarrow \frac{2x+6}{x^2+6x} = \frac{1}{4}$$

$$\Rightarrow x^2 + 6x = 8x + 24$$
$$\Rightarrow x^2 - 2x - 24 = 0$$
$$\Rightarrow x^2 - 6x + 4x - 24 = 0$$
$$\Rightarrow x(x-6) + 4(x-6) = 0$$
$$\Rightarrow (x-6)(x+4) = 0$$
$$\Rightarrow x = 6 \quad \text{or} \quad x = -4$$
$$\text{(taking +ve value)}$$

Hence, time taken by A alone to fill the cistern is 6 hours.

6. Net filling in 1 hour $= \left(\dfrac{1}{8} - \dfrac{1}{16} \right)$

$$= \frac{2-1}{16} = \frac{1}{16}$$

$\therefore$ Time taken to fill the cistern = 16 hours.

7. Net filling in 1 hour

$$= \left(\frac{1}{20} + \frac{1}{30} - \frac{1}{40} \right)$$

$$= \frac{6+4-3}{120} = \frac{7}{120}$$

$\therefore$ Time taken to fill the cistern

$$= \frac{120}{7} \text{ hrs} = 17\frac{1}{7} \text{ hrs.}$$

8. Work done by the leak in 1 hr

$$= \left(\frac{1}{8} - \frac{1}{10} \right) = \frac{5-4}{40} = \frac{1}{40}$$

So, the leak can empty the cistern in 40 hrs.

9. Part filled in 5 min by A and B

$$= 5\left(\frac{1}{20} + \frac{1}{25} \right) = \frac{9}{20}$$

Remaining part $= \left(1 - \dfrac{9}{20} \right) = \dfrac{11}{20}$

Now, $\dfrac{1}{20}$ part is filled by A in 1 minute.

$\therefore$ $\dfrac{11}{20}$ part will be filled by A in

$$\left(\frac{20 \times 11}{20} \right) \text{ min} = 11 \text{ min.}$$

10. Clearly, the rate of waste pipe is more, so the tank will be emptied, if both the pipes are opened.

Net work done by both the pipes in 1 minute.

$$= \left(\frac{1}{16} - \frac{1}{8} \right) = -\frac{1}{16}$$

(–ve sign means emptying)

So, both the pipes together will empty the full tank in 16 minutes. Hence, they will empty half full tank in 8 minutes.

11. Work done by waste pipe in 1 minute

$$= \frac{1}{10} + \frac{1}{15} - \frac{1}{18} = \frac{9+6-5}{90}$$

$$= \frac{10}{90} = \frac{1}{9}$$

$\therefore$ Waste pipe can empty the full cistern in 9 minutes.

12. Work done by both pipes in 1 hour

$$= \frac{1}{10} + \frac{1}{15} = \frac{3+2}{30} = \frac{5}{30} = \frac{1}{6}$$

So, both the pipes will fill it in 6 hours.

13. The part of the cistern filled by B in 17 min.

$$= \frac{1}{34} \times 17 = \frac{1}{2}$$

Remaining part $= 1 - \frac{1}{2} = \frac{1}{2}$

Time taken by A to fill the remaining part

$$= \frac{1/2}{1/20} = \frac{1}{2} \times \frac{20}{1} = 10 \text{ min.}$$

Hence, pipe A must be turned off after 10 minutes.

14. In 1 hour the part filled by both pipes

$$= \frac{1}{10} + \frac{1}{15} = \frac{3+2}{30} = \frac{5}{30} = \frac{1}{6}$$

Hence, both pipes can fill the tank in 6 hours.

15. In 1 hour the part emptied by the leak

$$= \frac{1}{8} - \frac{1}{10} = \frac{5-4}{40} = \frac{1}{40}$$

Hence, the leak can empty the full cistern in 40 hours.

16. Let x and $3x$ minutes taken by the two pipes respectively to fill the tank, then

$$\frac{1}{x} + \frac{1}{3x} = \frac{1}{36}$$

$$\Rightarrow \quad \frac{4}{3x} = \frac{1}{36}$$

$$\Rightarrow \quad 3x = 4 \times 36$$

$$\Rightarrow \quad x = \frac{4 \times 36}{3}$$

$$\Rightarrow \quad x = 48$$

Hence, time taken by slower pipe $= 3 \times 48 = 144$ minutes to fill the tank.

17. Let the tanker can be filled in x minutes, then

$$\frac{x}{2}\left(\frac{1}{60} + \frac{1}{40}\right) + \frac{x}{2} \times \frac{1}{40} = 1$$

$$\Rightarrow \quad \frac{x}{2}\left(\frac{1}{60} + \frac{2}{40}\right) = 1$$

$$\Rightarrow \quad \frac{x}{2}\left(\frac{2+6}{120}\right) = 1$$

$$\Rightarrow \quad \frac{x}{2} \times \frac{8}{120} = 1$$

$$\Rightarrow \quad \frac{x}{30} = 1$$

$$\Rightarrow \quad x = 30 \text{ minutes.}$$

18. In 30 minutes the part filled by pipe A

$$= 30 \times \frac{2}{75} = \frac{4}{5}$$

The remaining part $= 1 - \frac{4}{5} = \frac{1}{5}$

The time taken by pipe B to fill the remaining part

$$= \frac{1/5}{1/45} = \frac{1}{5} \times \frac{45}{1}$$

$$= 9 \text{ minutes.}$$

19. In 18 minutes the part filled by

pipe A $= 18 \times \dfrac{1}{24} = \dfrac{3}{4}$

Remaining part $= 1 - \dfrac{3}{4} = \dfrac{1}{4}$

Time taken by B to fill the remaining part

$$= \frac{1/4}{1/32} = \frac{1}{4} \times \frac{32}{1} = 8 \text{ minutes.}$$

20. In one minute the part emptied by both the pipes

$$= \frac{1}{6} - \frac{1}{10} = \frac{5-3}{30} = \frac{2}{30} = \frac{1}{15}$$

Time taken by both the pipes to empty $\dfrac{2}{5}$ tank

$$= \frac{2/5}{1/15} = \frac{2}{5} \times \frac{15}{1} = 6 \text{ minutes.}$$

16

EXPONENTS

1. What is the value of $a^5 \times a^7$?
   A. a^{35} B. a^2
   C. a^{12} D. $a^{5/7}$

2. Third power of 4 is equivalent to:
   A. 64 B. 81
   C. 12 D. 49

3. What is the difference between the third power of 2 and the second power of 3?
   A. 2 B. 5
   C. 3 D. 1

4. If $\sqrt{2^n} = 64$, the value of n is :
   A. 8 B. 4
   C. 12 D. 16

5. If $10^{2/5} \times 10^{8/5} = 10^n$, the value of n is :
   A. 2 B. 3
   C. 6 D. 4

6. The value of $27^3 \times 3^4 \div 3^{10}$ is equal to:
   A. 9 B. 27
   C. 81 D. $\dfrac{1}{27}$

7. The value of $6a^3b^3c^2 \div 2ab^2c$ is:
   A. $3a^2bc$ B. $3ab^2c$
   C. $3a^2b^2c^2$ D. $3a^3b^3c^3$

8. The expression $\dfrac{(-1)^{132}}{5^{-1}+3^{-1}}$ is equivalent to:

   A. $\dfrac{16}{9}$ B. $\dfrac{-15}{8}$
   C. $\dfrac{15}{8}$ D. $\dfrac{17}{8}$

9. $\left(x^{2/3}\right)^{-3/4}$ is equivalent to:
   A. $\dfrac{1}{x}$ B. $\dfrac{1}{\sqrt{x}}$
   C. $\dfrac{1}{x^2}$ D. $\dfrac{1}{x^{-2}}$

10. The value of $\left(-\dfrac{1}{125}\right)^{-2/3}$ is:
    A. $\dfrac{1}{25}$ B. 25
    C. 5 D. $\dfrac{1}{5}$

11. The positive exponential function of $\dfrac{a^{-3} \cdot a^{-4}}{a^{-5}}$ is:
    A. a^2 B. $\dfrac{1}{a^3}$
    C. $\dfrac{1}{a^4}$ D. $\dfrac{1}{a^2}$

12. $\sqrt[3]{x^6} \div \sqrt[6]{x^{12}} \times x^{-3} \times \sqrt[3]{x^9}$ is equivalent to :
    A. $2x$ B. 1
    C. $\dfrac{1}{3x^2}$ D. $\dfrac{1}{x}$

13. The value of $\left(\dfrac{2^3}{3^2}\right)^{2/3} \times \left(\dfrac{3^3}{2^2}\right)^{2/3}$

is :

A. $6^{4/3}$ B. $8^{2/3}$
C. $6^{2/3}$ D. $9^{1/3}$

14. The value of $\dfrac{x^{-2} \cdot y^{-4}}{x^{-3} \cdot y^{-1}} \div \dfrac{y^{-2}}{x^{-1}}$ is:

A. y B. $\dfrac{1}{y}$

C. xy D. $\dfrac{1}{xy}$

15. If $\sqrt{4^3} \times (4)^{3/2} \div 4^{-3} = 2^x$, the value of x will be:

A. 16 B. 8
C. 12 D. 4

16. $\dfrac{3^{n+3} - 3^{n+1} + 3^n}{2(3^{n-1})} + 2^{-1}$ is equivalent

to:

A. 32 B. 39
C. 35 D. 38

17. The value of $\sqrt[4]{256}$ is equal to:

A. 16 B. 4
C. 8 D. 64

18. $\left(\dfrac{1}{216}\right)^{-\frac{2}{3}} \div \left(\dfrac{1}{27}\right)^{-\frac{4}{3}} = ?$

A. $\dfrac{3}{4}$ B. $\dfrac{2}{3}$

C. $\dfrac{4}{9}$ D. $\dfrac{1}{8}$

19. If $\left(\sqrt{2}\right)^7 \times 8^2 = 2^y \times 2\sqrt{2}$ then the value of y is:

A. 16 B. 6
C. 8 D. 4

20. $(6.5 \times 6.5 - 45.5 + 3.5 \times 3.5)$ is equal to:

A. 10 B. 9
C. 7 D. 6

ANSWERS

1	2	3	4	5	6	7	8	9	10
C	A	D	C	A	B	A	C	B	B

11	12	13	14	15	16	17	18	19	20
D	B	C	B	C	D	B	C	C	B

EXPLANATORY ANSWERS

1. $a^5 \times a^7 = a^{5+7} = a^{12}$

$$\left[\because a^m \times a^n = a^{m+n}\right]$$

2. $(4)^3 = 4 \times 4 \times 4 = 64$
Hence third power of 4 is equivalent to 64.

3. Third power of $2 = 2^3$
$= 2 \times 2 \times 2 = 8$
and second power of $3 = 3^2$

$= 3 \times 3 = 9$
Difference $= 9 - 8 = 1$

4. $\sqrt{2^n} = 64 \implies 2^n = (64)^2$
$\implies (2)^n = (2^6)^2 = (2)^{12}$
$\implies n = 12.$

5. $10^{2/5} \times 10^{8/5} = 10^n$
$\implies 10^{2/5 + 8/5} = 10^n$
$\implies 10^{10/5} = 10^n$

$\Rightarrow \quad 10^2 = 10^n$

$\Rightarrow \qquad n = 2.$

6. $27^3 \times 3^4 \div 3^{10}$

$$= \left(3^3\right)^3 \times 3^4 \div 3^{10}$$

$$= 3^9 \times 3^4 \div 3^{10} = 3^{13-10}$$

$$= 3^3 = 3 \times 3 \times 3 = 27$$

7. $\dfrac{6a^3b^3c^2}{2ab^2c} = 3a^2bc.$

8. $\because \quad \dfrac{(-1)^{132}}{5^{-1}+3^{-1}} = \dfrac{\left((-1)^2\right)^{66}}{5^{-1}+3^{-1}}$

$$= \dfrac{1^{66}}{\dfrac{1}{5}+\dfrac{1}{3}} = \dfrac{1}{\dfrac{3+5}{15}}$$

$$= \dfrac{1}{\dfrac{8}{15}} = \dfrac{1}{8} \times \dfrac{15}{1} = \dfrac{15}{8}.$$

9. $\left(x^{\frac{2}{3}}\right)^{-\frac{3}{4}} = x^{\left(\frac{2}{3}\right)\left(-\frac{3}{4}\right)}$

$$= x^{-\frac{1}{2}} = \dfrac{1}{x^{\frac{1}{2}}} = \dfrac{1}{\sqrt{x}}$$

10. $\left(-\dfrac{1}{125}\right)^{-\frac{2}{3}} = \dfrac{1}{\left(-\dfrac{1}{125}\right)^{\frac{2}{3}}}$

$$= (-125)^{\frac{2}{3}}$$

$$= (-5)^{3 \times \frac{2}{3}} = (-5)^2 = 25.$$

11. $\dfrac{a^{-3} \times a^{-4}}{a^{-5}} = \dfrac{a^{-7}}{a^{-5}}$

$$= a^{-7+5} = a^{-2} = \dfrac{1}{a^2}$$

12. $x^{6/3} \div x^{12/6} \times x^{-3} \times x^{9/3}$

$$= x^2 \div x^2 \times x^{-3} \times x^3$$

$$= x^{2-2-3+3} = x^0 = 1.$$

13. $\left(\dfrac{2^3}{3^2}\right)^{\frac{2}{3}} \times \left(\dfrac{3^3}{2^2}\right)^{\frac{2}{3}}$

$$= \left(\dfrac{2^3}{3^2} \times \dfrac{3^3}{2^2}\right)^{\frac{2}{3}} = \left(2^{3-2} \times 3^{3-2}\right)^{\frac{2}{3}}$$

$$= (2 \times 3)^{\frac{2}{3}} = (6)^{\frac{2}{3}}.$$

14. $\left(\dfrac{x^3}{x^2} \times \dfrac{y^1}{y^4}\right) \div \dfrac{x^1}{y^2}$

$$= \dfrac{x}{y^3} \times \dfrac{y^2}{x^1} = \dfrac{x^{1-1}}{y^{3-2}} = \dfrac{x^0}{y^1} = \dfrac{1}{y}.$$

15. $\because \quad \sqrt{4^3} \times 4^{\frac{3}{2}} \div 4^{-3} = 2^x$

$$\Rightarrow \dfrac{4^{\frac{3}{2}} \times 4^{\frac{3}{2}}}{4^{-3}} = 2^x$$

$$\Rightarrow \dfrac{4^3}{4^{-3}} = 2^x \quad \Rightarrow \quad 4^6 = 2^x$$

$$\Rightarrow (2^2)^6 = (2)^x$$

$$\Rightarrow 2^{12} = 2^x \quad \Rightarrow \quad x = 12$$

$\therefore$ Value of $x = 12.$

16. $\because \quad \dfrac{3^{n+3} - 3^{n+1} + 3^n}{2(3^{n-1})} + 2^{-1}$

$$= \dfrac{3^n \cdot 3^3 - 3^n \cdot 3 + 3^n}{2 \cdot 3^n \cdot 3^{-1}} + 2^{-1}$$

$$= \dfrac{3^3 - 3 + 1}{2 \cdot 3^{-1}} + 2^{-1}$$

$$= \dfrac{3^4 - 3^2 + 3}{2} + \dfrac{1}{2}$$

$$= \dfrac{81 - 9 + 3}{2} + \dfrac{1}{2} = \dfrac{76}{2} = 38.$$

17. $\sqrt[4]{256} = (256)^{\frac{1}{4}} = (4^4)^{\frac{1}{4}} = 4.$

18. $\left(\dfrac{1}{216}\right)^{-\frac{2}{3}} \div \left(\dfrac{1}{27}\right)^{-\frac{4}{3}}$

$$= (216)^{\frac{2}{3}} \div (27)^{\frac{4}{3}}$$

$$= (6^3)^{\times \frac{2}{3}} \div (3^3)^{\frac{4}{3}}$$

$$= 6^2 \div 3^4 = \frac{6 \times 6}{3 \times 3 \times 3 \times 3} = \frac{4}{9}.$$

19. $(\sqrt{2})^7 \times 8^2 = 2^y \times 2\sqrt{2}$

$\Rightarrow (\sqrt{2})^{6+1} \times (2^3)^2 = 2^y \times 2\sqrt{2}$

$\Rightarrow (\sqrt{2})^6 \times \sqrt{2} \times 2^6 = 2^y \times 2\sqrt{2}$

$\Rightarrow 2^{3+6}\sqrt{2} = 2^y \times 2\sqrt{2}$

$\Rightarrow 2^9 = 2^y \times 2$

$\Rightarrow \dfrac{2^9}{2} = 2^y$

$\Rightarrow 2^8 = 2^y \Rightarrow y = 8.$

20. $(6.5 \times 6.5 - 45.5 + 3.5 \times 3.5)$

$= (6.5)^2 - 2\,(6.5)(3.5) + (3.5)^2$

$= (6.5 - 3.5)^2$

$\qquad [(a - b)^2 = a^2 - 2ab + b^2]$

$= (3)^2 = 3 \times 3 = 9.$

PROBABILITY

1. A dice is thrown once. Find the probability of getting a number greater than 3.

   A. $\dfrac{2}{3}$ B. $\dfrac{1}{3}$

   C. $\dfrac{1}{2}$ D. $\dfrac{3}{2}$

2. A bag contains 5 Red balls, 8 White balls, 4 Green balls and 7 Black balls. If one ball is drawn at random, find the probability that it is Black.

   A. $\dfrac{7}{24}$ B. $\dfrac{5}{24}$

   C. $\dfrac{5}{6}$ D. $\dfrac{1}{4}$

3. Find the probability that a number selected from the numbers 1 to 25 is not a prime number when each of the given number is equally to be selected.

   A. $\dfrac{9}{25}$ B. $\dfrac{16}{25}$

   C. $\dfrac{21}{25}$ D. $\dfrac{14}{25}$

4. A bag contains 3 Red balls and 5 Black balls. A ball is drawn at random from the bag. What is the probability that the ball drawn is not Red?

   A. $\dfrac{3}{8}$ B. $\dfrac{5}{8}$

   C. $\dfrac{1}{8}$ D. $\dfrac{7}{8}$

5. A card is drawn at random from a well-shuffled deck of playing cards. Find the probability that the card drawn is a card of spade or an ace.

   A. $\dfrac{11}{13}$ B. $\dfrac{1}{26}$

   C. $\dfrac{4}{13}$ D. $\dfrac{9}{13}$

6. If a letter is chosen at random from the word TRIANGLE.

   What is the probability that it a vowel?

   A. $\dfrac{3}{8}$ B. $\dfrac{5}{8}$

   C. $\dfrac{1}{4}$ D. $\dfrac{3}{4}$

7. What is the chance that a leap year, selected at random, will contain 53 Sundays?

   A. $\dfrac{52}{365}$ B. $\dfrac{52}{366}$

   C. $\dfrac{2}{7}$ D. $\dfrac{5}{7}$

8. A die is thrown once. Find the probability of getting an even number.

   A. $\dfrac{1}{3}$ B. $\dfrac{1}{2}$

   C. $\dfrac{1}{4}$ D. $\dfrac{1}{6}$

9. Two friends were born in the year 2000. What is the probability that they have the same birthday?

   A. $\dfrac{1}{500}$ B. $\dfrac{1}{730}$

   C. $\dfrac{1}{365}$ D. $\dfrac{1}{366}$

10. The probability that a number selected at random from the set of numbers (1, 2, 3, 4, ... 100) is a cube is:

   A. $\dfrac{1}{25}$ B. $\dfrac{2}{25}$

   C. $\dfrac{3}{25}$ D. $\dfrac{4}{25}$

11. In a cricket match, a batsman hits boundary 8 times out of 40 balls he plays. Find the probability that he did not hit boundary.

   A. 0.8   B. 0.6

   C. 0.5   D. 0.4

12. Three unbiased coins are tossed. What is the probability of getting at least 2 heads?

   A. $\dfrac{1}{4}$ B. $\dfrac{1}{2}$

   C. $\dfrac{1}{3}$ D. $\dfrac{1}{8}$

13. In a simultaneous throw of two dice, what is the probability of getting a total of 7?

14. What is the probability of getting a sum 9 from two throws of a dice?

   A. $\dfrac{1}{6}$ B. $\dfrac{1}{8}$

   C. $\dfrac{1}{9}$ D. $\dfrac{1}{12}$

15. Tickets numbered 1 to 20 are mixed up and then a ticket drawn at random. What is the probability that the ticket drawn bears a number which is a multiple of 3?

   A. $\dfrac{3}{10}$ B. $\dfrac{3}{20}$

   C. $\dfrac{2}{5}$ D. $\dfrac{1}{2}$

16. A card is drawn from a pack of 52 cards. The probability of getting a queen of club or a king of heart is:

   A. $\dfrac{1}{13}$ B. $\dfrac{2}{13}$

   C. $\dfrac{1}{26}$ D. $\dfrac{1}{52}$

17. Two cards are drawn together from a pack of 52 cards. The probability that one is a spade and one is a heart is:

   A. $\dfrac{3}{20}$ B. $\dfrac{29}{34}$

   C. $\dfrac{47}{100}$ D. $\dfrac{13}{102}$

Above (Q.13 options appear with Q.8 layout):

   A. $\dfrac{1}{6}$ B. $\dfrac{1}{4}$

   C. $\dfrac{2}{3}$ D. $\dfrac{3}{4}$

18. A bag contains 6 white and 4 red balls. Three balls are drawn at random. What is the probability that one ball is red and the other two are white?

A. $\dfrac{1}{2}$ B. $\dfrac{1}{12}$

C. $\dfrac{3}{10}$ D. $\dfrac{7}{12}$

19. A box contains 20 electric bulbs, out of which 4 are defective. Two bulbs are chosen at random from this box. The probability that at least one of these is defective, is:

A. $\dfrac{4}{19}$ B. $\dfrac{7}{19}$

C. $\dfrac{12}{19}$ D. $\dfrac{21}{95}$

20. Two dice are tossed. The probability that the total score is a prime number is:

A. $\dfrac{1}{6}$ B. $\dfrac{5}{12}$

C. $\dfrac{1}{2}$ D. $\dfrac{7}{9}$

ANSWERS

1	2	3	4	5	6	7	8	9	10
C	A	B	B	C	A	C	B	D	A

11	12	13	14	15	16	17	18	19	20
A	B	A	C	A	C	D	A	B	B

EXPLANATORY ANSWERS

1. Sample space S = {1, 2, 3, 4, 5, 6};
$n(S) = 6$

Let A = "getting a number greater than 3", then

A = {4, 5, 6}; $n(A) = 3$

$$P(A) = \dfrac{n(A)}{n(S)} = \dfrac{3}{6} = \dfrac{1}{2}$$

2. Total balls = 5 + 8 + 4 + 7 = 24

$$P(\text{Black}) = \dfrac{7}{24}$$

3. We are given numbers from 1 to 25

$n(S) = 25$

Prime numbers from 1 to 25 are 2, 3, 5, 7, 11, 13, 17, 19, 23.

These are 9 prime numbers.

Let E denote the event 'Number drawn is not prime'

$\therefore n(E) = 25 - 9 = 16$

$$P(E) = \dfrac{16}{25}.$$

4. Total number of balls in the bag
= 3 + 5 = 8

Let E denote the event 'Ball drawn is Red'

$\therefore n(E) = 3$ and $n(S) = 8$

(*i*) $P(E) = \dfrac{n(E)}{n(S)} = \dfrac{3}{8}$

(*ii*) P (not red) = $P(\bar{E})$

$= 1 - P(E) = 1 - \dfrac{3}{8} = \dfrac{5}{8}.$

5. There are 52 cards in a deck of 52 playing cards. There are 13 spades and 4 aces in 52 playing cards. Out of 13 spades there is one ace.

$\therefore$ Favourable no ways for the card drawn to be spade or an ace

$$= 13 \text{ spades} + 3 \text{ aces} = 16$$

$\therefore$ p(a card of spade or an ace)

$$= \frac{16}{52} = \frac{4}{13}.$$

6. Since there are three vowels out of a total of 8 letters, the probability of choosing a vowel is $\frac{3}{8}$.

7. A leap year has 366 days. In a leap year, here are 52 complete weeks (52 Sundays) and 2 days over these two days can be as follows.

Sunday and Monday, Monday and Tuesday, Tuesday and Wednesday, Wednesday and Thursday, Thursday and Friday, Friday and Saturday, Saturday and Sunday.

Out of these 7 possibilities, only two (Saturday and Sunday; Sunday and Monday are favourable for having 53 Sundays)

Required chance $= \dfrac{2}{7}$

8. A die is thrown once. Its sample space is

$$S = \{1, 2, 3, 4, 5, 6\},$$
$$n(S) = 6$$

Let E be an even number, then

$$E = \{2, 4, 6\}$$

Number of favourable cases

$$= n(E) = 3$$

$\therefore$ $p(E) = \dfrac{n(E)}{n(S)} = \dfrac{3}{6} = \dfrac{1}{2}.$

9. Year 2000 is a leap year. There are 366 days in the year 2000. Total number of cases in which two friends can be born on the same day are 366.

Out of 366 days, number of favourable ways in which two friends have the same birth day = 1

$\therefore$ Required probability $= \dfrac{1}{366}.$

10. From the natural numbers 1 to 100 the four number 1, 8, 27 and 64 are cubes

$\therefore$ Required probability

$$= \frac{4}{100} = \frac{1}{25}$$

11. Let A denote the event that the batsman did not hit a boundary.

We have, total number of trials $= 40$

Number of trials in which the event A happened $= 40 - 8 = 32$

$\therefore$ P(A) $= \dfrac{32}{40} = \dfrac{4}{5} = 0.8.$

12. Here S = {HH, HT, TH, TT}

Let E = Event of getting at least one head

$$= \{HT, TH, HH\}$$

$\therefore$ P(E) $= \dfrac{n(E)}{n(S)} = \dfrac{4}{8} = \dfrac{1}{2}.$

13. We know that in a simultaneous through of two dice,

$n(S) = 6 \times 6 = 36$

Let E = Event of getting a total of

$7 = \{(1, 6), (2, 5), (3, 4), (4, 3),$ $(5, 2), (6, 1)\}$

$$\therefore P(E) = \frac{n(E)}{n(S)} = \frac{6}{36} = \frac{1}{6}.$$

14. In two throws of a die,

$$n(S) = 6 \times 6 = 36$$

Let E = Event of getting a sum 9

$$= \{(3, 6), (4, 5), (5, 4), (6, 3)\}$$

$$\therefore P(E) = \frac{n(E)}{n(S)} = \frac{4}{36} = \frac{1}{9}.$$

15. Here, S = (1, 2, 3, ... 19, 20)

Let E = Event of getting a multiple of 3

$$= \{3, 6, 9, 12, 15, 18\}$$

$$\therefore P(E) = \frac{n(E)}{n(S)} = \frac{6}{20} = \frac{3}{10}$$

16. Here, $n(S) = 52$

Let E = Event of getting a queen of club or a king of heart.

Then, $n(E) = 2$

$$\therefore P(E) = \frac{n(E)}{n(S)} = \frac{2}{52} = \frac{1}{26}.$$

17. Let S be the sample space. Then,

$$n(S) = {}^{52}C_2 = \frac{52 \times 51}{2 \times 1} = 1326$$

Let E = Event of getting 1 spade and 1 heart.

$\therefore n(E)$ = Number of ways of choosing 1 spade out of 13 and 1 heart out of 13

$$({}^{13}C_1 \times {}^{13}C_2) = (13 \times 13)$$
$$= 169$$

$$\therefore P(E) = \frac{n(E)}{n(S)} = \frac{169}{1326} = \frac{13}{102}.$$

18. Let S be the sample space. Then

$n(S)$ = Number of ways of drawing 3 balls out of 10

$$= {}^{10}C_3 = \frac{10 \times 9 \times 8}{3 \times 2 \times 1} = 120$$

Let E = Event of drawing 1 red and 2 white balls.

$\therefore n(E)$ = Number of ways of drawing 1 red ball out of 4 and 2 white balls out of 6.

$$= ({}^{4}C_1 \times {}^{6}C_2) = \left(\frac{4 \times 6 \times 5}{2 \times 1}\right)$$
$$= 60$$

$$\therefore P(E) = \frac{n(E)}{n(S)} = \frac{60}{120} = \frac{1}{2}.$$

19. P(None of defective)

$$= \frac{{}^{16}C_2}{{}^{20}C_2}$$

$$= \left(\frac{16 \times 15}{2 \times 1} \times \frac{2 \times 1}{20 \times 19}\right) = \frac{12}{19}$$

P(at least one is defective)

$$= \left(1 - \frac{12}{19}\right) = \frac{7}{19}$$

20. Clearly, $n(S) = (6 \times 6) = 36$

Let E = Event that the sum is a prime number. Then,

$E = \{(1, 1), (1, 2), (1, 4), (1, 6), (2, 1),$ $(2, 3), (2, 5), (3, 2), (3, 4), (4, 1),$ $(4, 3), (5, 2), (5, 6), (6, 1), (6, 5)\}$

$$\therefore n(E) = 15$$

$$\therefore P(E) = \frac{n(E)}{n(S)} = \frac{15}{36} = \frac{5}{12}$$

18

MEASURES OF CENTRAL TENDENCY

1. Find the mean weight of 7 students of a school, having their weight in kg 40, 42, 38, 50, 62, 54, 50.
   A. 48
   B. 50
   C. 54
   D. 42

2. Calculate the mean of the following
   2256, 2214, 2220, 2234, 2240, 2238, 2224, 2230.
   A. 2240
   B. 2220
   C. 2232
   D. 2234

3. The median of the following 45, 65, 60, 70, 55, 69, 80, 54, 84 is:
   A. 55
   B. 65
   C. 60
   D. 70

4. Find the median of the following 6, 5, 20, 3, 14, 13, 4, 7, 9, 15
   A. 14
   B. 13
   C. 9
   D. 8

5. Find the mode of the following 12, 21, 25, 24, 20, 21, 23, 12, 21, 36, 40, 21, 7
   A. 21
   B. 12
   C. 23
   D. 20

6. The mean of the positive integers from 1 to 10 is:
   A. 4.5
   B. 5.5
   C. 6.5
   D. 5.8

7. If the mean of 2, 5, a and 7 is 6 then value of a is:
   A. 8
   B. 6
   C. 10
   D. 7

8. Find the mode of 2, 2, 3, 4, 4, 3, 3, 5, 2, 2, 1, 1.
   A. 1
   B. 3
   C. 4
   D. 2

9. The median of 6, 12, 30, 14, 18, 25, 28, 22, 20, 25 is:
   A. 21
   B. 22
   C. 25
   D. 18

10. The mean of first-five natural numbers is:
    A. 2
    B. 4
    C. 3
    D. 5

11. Find the median of the following 20, 27, 22, 12, 17, 25 and 18.
    A. 22
    B. 20
    C. 12
    D. 18

12. What is the frequency of 3 in the following frequency distribution: 3, 7, 0, 5, 3, 2, 3, 4, 3, 2, 7, 8, 3, 3
    A. 6
    B. 3
    C. 2
    D. 5

13. Median for the set of numbers 9, 10, 14, 16 and 18 is:
    A. 10
    B. 14
    C. 16
    D. 15

14. Find the median of the following marks obtained by 12 students in a class-test marked out of 50 marks:

25, 32, 35, 19, 23, 30, 16, 20, 22, 15, 13, 27

A. 17.5   B. 22.5
C. 21   D. 23

15. Mode for the set of numbers 3, 2, 3, 4, 5, 3, 3, 2, 1, 1 is:

A. 4   B. 2
C. 3   D. 1

16. The arithmetic mean of the positive integers from 1 to 20 is:

A. 10.5   B. 12.5
C. 18.6   D. 11.5

17. If the arithmetic mean of 10, 12, x, 8 and 20 is 11, the value of x is:

A. 4   B. 8
C. 12   D. 5

18. Arithmetic mean of 5 numbers is 21. If a number 33 is included, then the new mean is:

A. 23   B. 21
C. 18   D. 32

19. The mode of 1, 1, 2, 2, 2, 3, 3, 3, 3, 4, 4, 4, 4, 4 is:

A. 2   B. 3
C. 4   D. 1

20. If the mean of 6, 4, 7, P and 10 is 8, then the value of P is:

A. 13   B. 8
C. 10   D. 6

ANSWERS

1	2	3	4	5	6	7	8	9	10
A	C	B	D	A	B	C	D	A	C

11	12	13	14	15	16	17	18	19	20
B	D	B	B	C	A	D	A	C	A

EXPLANATORY ANSWERS

1. Mean weight

$$= \frac{40+42+38+50+62+54+50}{7}$$

$$= \frac{336}{7} = 48 \text{ kg.}$$

2. Mean

$$= \frac{\begin{array}{c}2256+2214+2220+2234\\+2240+2238+2224+2230\end{array}}{8}$$

$$= \frac{17856}{8} = 2232$$

3. First write in ascending order

45, 54, 55, 60, 65, 69, 70, 80, 84

Here, $n = 9$ which is odd number.

$$\therefore \text{Median} = \left(\frac{9+1}{2}\right)^{th} \text{ term}$$

$$= 5\text{th term} = 65.$$

4. First write in ascending order

3, 4, 5, 6, 7, 9, 13, 14, 15, 20

Here, $n = 10$, which is even number. Hence, there are two central terms.

$i.e.,$ $\left(\dfrac{10}{2}\right)^{th}$ and $\left(\dfrac{10}{2}+1\right)^{th}$ terms

$\therefore$ Median $= \dfrac{\text{Value of 5th term} + \text{Value of 6th term}}{2}$

$= \dfrac{7+9}{2} = \dfrac{16}{2} = 8.$

5. In the given set of numbers 21 occurs maximum number of times. *i.e.*, 4 times.
   Hence, the required mode is 21.

6. Mean $= \dfrac{1+2+3+4+5+6+7+8+9+10}{10}$

   $= \dfrac{55}{10} = 5.5$

7. Mean $= \dfrac{2+5+a+7}{4}$

   $\Rightarrow \quad 6 = \dfrac{a+14}{4}$

   $\Rightarrow a + 14 = 24$

   $\Rightarrow \quad a = 24 - 14 = 10$

   $\therefore$ Value of $a = 10$.

8. In the given set of numbers 2 occurs maximum number of times, i.e., 4 times.
   Hence, mode is 2.

9. On arranging the given numbers in ascending order, we get following series:
   6, 12, 14, 18, 20, 22, 25, 25, 28, 30
   Here, $n = 10$ which is even number.

   $\therefore$ Median $= \dfrac{\text{Value of 5th term} + \text{Value of 6th term}}{2}$

   $= \dfrac{20+22}{2} = \dfrac{42}{2} = 21.$

10. First five natural numbers are 1, 2, 3, 4 and 5

    Mean $= \dfrac{1+2+3+4+5}{5}$

    $= \dfrac{15}{5} = 3$

11. First write in ascending order, we have the following number series:
    12, 17, 18, 20 , 22, 25 and 27
    Here, $n = 7$ which is odd number

    $\therefore \quad$ Median $= \left(\dfrac{n+1}{2}\right)^{th}$ term

    $= \left(\dfrac{7+1}{2}\right)^{th}$ term

    $= $ 4th term

    $= 20.$

12. In the given distribution 3 occurs 5 times.
    Hence, frequency will be 5.

13. On arranging the given numbers in ascending order, we have,
    9, 10, 14, 16, 18
    Since value of mid-term $= 14$
    $\therefore$ Median $= 14.$

14. On arranging the marks obtained by the students in ascending order, we get following set of numbers:
    13, 15, 16, 19, 20, 22, 23, 25, 27, 30, 32, 35
    Here, $n = 12$ which is even number

    Median $= \dfrac{\text{6th term} + \text{7th term}}{2}$

    $= \dfrac{22+23}{2} = \dfrac{45}{2} = 22.5.$

15. In the given set of numbers 3 occurs maximum number of times, i.e., four times. Hence mode is 3.

16. Positive integers from 1 to 20 are

1, 2, 3, 4, ... 20.

$$\text{Mean} = \frac{1+2+3+.......+20}{20}$$

$$= \frac{20 \times 21}{2 \times 20} = \frac{21}{2} = 10.5.$$

$$\left[\because \text{ Sum of first } n \text{ natural numbers} = \frac{n(n+1)}{2} \right]$$

17. $\text{Mean} = \dfrac{10+12+x+8+20}{5}$

$$\Rightarrow \quad 11 = \frac{x+50}{5}$$

$$\Rightarrow \quad x + 50 = 55$$

$$\Rightarrow \quad x = 55 - 50 = 5$$

$\therefore$ Value of $x = 5$.

18. Sum of 5 numbers $= 21 \times 5$

$$= 105$$

increased number $= 33$

Sum of 6 numbers $= 105 + 33$

$$= 138$$

$$\text{New mean} = \frac{138}{6} = 23.$$

19. Since 4 occurs maximum number of times, i.e., five times $\therefore$ Mode is 4.

20. $\text{Mean} = \dfrac{6+4+7+P+10}{5}$

$$\Rightarrow \quad 8 = \frac{P+27}{5}$$

$$\Rightarrow \quad P + 27 = 40$$

$$\Rightarrow \quad P = 40 - 27 = 13.$$

19

ALGEBRA

1. If $x + \dfrac{1}{x} = 15$, then, the value of $x^2 + \dfrac{1}{x^2}$ will be:

   A. 228   B. 230
   C. 323   D. 223

2. If $x = 12$ and $y = 4$, the value of $(x+y)^{x/y}$ will be:

   A. 4096   B. 3896
   C. 4196   D. 5086

3. If $x = 9, y = \sqrt{17}$, then the value of $\left(x^2 - y^2\right)^{-1/2}$ will be:

   A. 2^{-4} B. 2^2
   C. 3^{-3} D. 2^{-3}

4. What should be added to $\dfrac{x}{y}$ to get $\dfrac{y}{x}$?

   A. $\dfrac{x^2 - y^2}{xy}$ B. $\dfrac{y^2 - x^2}{xy}$
   C. $\dfrac{2xy}{x^2 - y^2}$ D. $\dfrac{y^2 - x^2}{2xy}$

5. If $x + y = 2z$, then the value of $\left(\dfrac{x}{x-z} + \dfrac{z}{y-z}\right)$ will be:

   A. 1   B. 4
   C. 3/2   D. 2

6. If $x + y + z = 0$, then the value of $\dfrac{(x+y)(y+z)(z+x)}{xyz}$ will be:

   A. –3   B. –2
   C. 0   D. –1

7. If $x + \dfrac{1}{x} = 3$, the value of $x^4 + \dfrac{1}{x^4}$ will be:

   A. 49   B. 47
   C. 37   D. 42

8. If $\left(x + \dfrac{1}{x}\right)^2 = 0$, then the value of $\left(x^2 + \dfrac{1}{x^2}\right)$ will be:

   A. 1   B. –1
   C. 2   D. –2

9. If $\left(a + \dfrac{2}{a}\right) = 3$, then the value of $\left(a - \dfrac{2}{a}\right)$ will be:

   A. ± 4 B. ± 5
   C. ± 2 D. ± 1

10. If $\sqrt{a} + \dfrac{1}{\sqrt{a}} = 4$, then the value of $a^2 + \dfrac{1}{a^2}$ will be:

    A. 194   B. 199
    C. 178   D. 192

11. If $x^2 + y^2 + z^2 = 115$ and $xy + yz + zx = 27$, then the value of $x + y + z$ will be:

A. ± 15 B. ± 13
C. ± 17 D. ± 19

12. If $x = 17$, $y = 15$ and $z = 13$, then the value of $x^2 + y^2 + z^2 - 2xy - 2xz - 2yz$ will be:

A. 111   B. 109
C. 121   D. 120

13. If $x + y = 1$, then the value of $x^3 + y^3 + 3xy$ will be:

A. 1   B. 4
C. 3   D. 7

14. What will be the value of $x^3 + y^3 + z^3 - 3xyz$ if $x + y + z = 16$ and $xy + yz + zx = 78$?

A. 352   B. 452
C. 342   D. 360

15. Which of the following is equivalent to $(x^4 + y^4)(x^2 + y^2)(x + y)(x - y)$?

A. $x^8 - y^8$ B. $x^{10} - y^{10}$
C. $x^6 - y^6$ D. $x^{12} - y^{12}$

16. $(x^{b+c})^{b-c} \cdot (x^{c+a})^{c-a} \cdot (x^{a+b})^{a-b}$ is equivalent to:

A. 0   B. x^{a+b+c}
C. $x^{a^2+b^2+c^2}$ D. 1

17. If $x - \dfrac{1}{x} = \sqrt{21}$, then the value of $\left(x^2 + \dfrac{1}{x^2} \right)\left(x + \dfrac{1}{x} \right)$ will be:

A. 120   B. 115
C. 119   D. 118

18. If $x^2 = y + z$, $y^2 = z + x$ and $z^2 = x + y$, then the value of $\left(\dfrac{1}{x+1} + \dfrac{1}{y+1} + \dfrac{1}{z+1} \right)$ will be?

A. 4   B. 3
C. 1   D. 2

19. If $a + b + c = 0$, then what will be the value of $\dfrac{1}{b^2 + c^2 - a^2} + \dfrac{1}{c^2 + a^2 - b^2} + \dfrac{1}{a^2 + b^2 - c^2}$?

A. 2   B. 1
C. 4   D. 0

20. If $a = x + y$, $b = x - y$ and $c = 2x - 1$, then the value of $a^2 + b^2 + c^2 - 2ab + 2ac - 2bc$ will be:

A. $(2y + 2x - 1)^2$ B. $(3y + 2x - 1)^2$
C. $(2y + 3x - 1)^2$ D. $(4y + 2x - 1)^2$

ANSWERS

1	2	3	4	5	6	7	8	9	10
D	A	D	B	A	D	B	D	D	A

11	12	13	14	15	16	17	18	19	20
B	C	A	A	A	D	B	C	D	A

EXPLANATORY ANSWERS

1. $\because x + \dfrac{1}{x} = 15 \Rightarrow \left(x + \dfrac{1}{x} \right)^2 = (15)^2$

$\Rightarrow x^2 + \dfrac{1}{x^2} + 2 \cdot x \cdot \dfrac{1}{x} = 225$

$\therefore x^2 + \dfrac{1}{x^2} = 225 - 2 = 223$.

2. $(x + y)^{x/y} = (12 + 4)^{12/4}$

$= (16)^3 = 4096$.   [$\because x = 12, y = 4$]

3. $\left(x^2 - y^2\right)^{-1/2} = (81-17)^{-1/2}$

$$= (64)^{-1/2} = \frac{1}{\sqrt{64}} = \frac{1}{8} = 2^{-3}.$$

4. Suppose A is added to $\dfrac{x}{y}$, then $\dfrac{x}{y}$

$$+ A = \frac{y}{x} \Rightarrow A = \frac{y}{x} - \frac{x}{y} = \frac{y^2 - x^2}{xy}$$

$\therefore$ when $\dfrac{y^2 - x^2}{xy}$ is added to $\dfrac{x}{y}$,

the sum so obtained will be $\dfrac{y}{x}$.

5. $\because x + y = 2z \Rightarrow x - z = z - y$
$$= -(y-z)$$

$$\therefore \frac{x}{x-z} + \frac{z}{y-z} = \frac{x}{-(y-z)} + \frac{z}{y-z}$$

$$= \frac{z-x}{y-z} = 1. \quad [\because x - z = z - y]$$

6. $\because \quad x + y + z = 0 \Rightarrow x + y = -z$
$$x + y + z = 0 \Rightarrow y + z = -x$$
and $x + y + z = 0 \Rightarrow z + x = -y$

$$\therefore \frac{(x+y)(y+z)(z+x)}{xyz} = \frac{-z.-x.-y}{xyz}$$

$$= -1.$$

7. $\because \quad x + \dfrac{1}{x} = 3 \Rightarrow \left(x + \dfrac{1}{x}\right)^2 = (3)^2$

$$\Rightarrow x^2 + \frac{1}{x^2} + 2.x.\frac{1}{x} = 9$$

$$\Rightarrow x^2 + \frac{1}{x^2} = 9 - 2 = 7$$

$$\because \quad x^2 + \frac{1}{x^2} = 7$$

$$\Rightarrow \left(x^2 + \frac{1}{x^2}\right)^2 = (7)^2$$

$$\Rightarrow x^4 + \frac{1}{x^4} + 2.x^2.\frac{1}{x^2} = 49$$

$$\therefore \quad x^4 + \frac{1}{x^4} = 49 - 2 = 47.$$

8. $\left(x + \dfrac{1}{x}\right)^2 = 0$

$$\Rightarrow x^2 + \frac{1}{x^2} + 2x.\frac{1}{x} = 0$$

$$\Rightarrow \qquad x^2 + \frac{1}{x^2} = -2.$$

9. $\because \left(a - \dfrac{2}{a}\right)^2 = \left(a + \dfrac{2}{a}\right)^2 - 4.a.\dfrac{2}{a}$

$$= (3)^2 - 8 = 9 - 8 = 1$$

$$\therefore \left(a - \frac{2}{a}\right) = \pm\sqrt{1} = \pm 1.$$

10. $\because \sqrt{a} + \dfrac{1}{\sqrt{a}} = 4 \Rightarrow \left(\sqrt{a} + \dfrac{1}{\sqrt{a}}\right)^2$

$$= (4)^2 = a + \frac{1}{a} + 2.\sqrt{a}.\frac{1}{\sqrt{a}} = 16$$

$$= 16 - 2 = 14$$

$$\because \left(a + \frac{1}{a}\right) = 14 \Rightarrow \left(a + \frac{1}{a}\right)^2 = (14)^2$$

$$\Rightarrow a^2 + \frac{1}{a^2} + 2.a.\frac{1}{a} = 196$$

$$\therefore a^2 + \frac{1}{a^2} = 196 - 2 = 194.$$

11. $\because (x + y + z)^2 = x^2 + y^2 + z^2$
$$+ 2(xy + yz + zx)$$
$$\therefore (x + y + z)^2 = 115 + 2 \times 27$$
$$= 115 + 54 = 169$$
$$\therefore (x + y + z) = \sqrt{169} = \pm 13.$$

12. The given expression is equivalent to $(x - y - z)^2$
$$\because (x - y - z)^2 = (17 - 15 - 13)^2$$
$$= (-11)^2 = 121.$$

13. $\because (x + y)^3 = x^3 + y^3 + 3xy(x + y)$
$$\therefore \qquad (1)^3 = x^3 + y^3 + 3xy \times 1$$
$$\therefore \qquad 1 = x^3 + y^3 + 3xy.$$

14. $\because$ $(x+y+z)=16$
$\Rightarrow (x+y+z)^2=(16)^2$
$= x^2+y^2+z^2+2(xy+yz+zx)=256$
$\therefore$ $x^2+y^2+z^2+2\times78=256$
$\Rightarrow x^2+y^2+z^2=256-156=100$
$\therefore$ $x^3+y^3+z^3-3xyz=(x+y+z)$
$[(x^2+y^2+z^2)-(xy+yz+zx)]$
$=16[100-78]=16\times22=352.$

15. $\because$ $(x^4+y^4)(x^2+y^2)(x+y)(x-y)$
$=(x^4+y^4)(x^2+y^2)(x^2-y^2)$
$=(x^4+y^4)(x^4-y^4)=x^8-y^8.$

16. $\because$ $(x^{b+c})^{b-c}=x^{(b+c)(b-c)}=x^{\left(b^2-c^2\right)}$

Similarly $(x^{c+a})^{c-a}=x^{\left(c^2-a^2\right)}$

and $(x^{(a+b)})^{(a-b)}=x^{\left(a^2-b^2\right)}$
$\therefore (x^{b+c})^{(b-c)}(x^{c+a})^{(c-a)}(x^{a+b})^{(a-b)}$
$=x^{b^2-c^2}.x^{c^2-a^2}.x^{a^2-b^2}$
$=x^{b^2-c^2+c^2-a^2+a^2-b^2}=x^0=1.$

17. $\because$ $\left(x+\dfrac{1}{x}\right)^2=\left(x-\dfrac{1}{x}\right)^2+4.x.\dfrac{1}{x}$

$=\left(\sqrt{21}\right)^2+4=21+4=25$

$\therefore \left(x+\dfrac{1}{x}\right)=\sqrt{25}=5$

$\therefore \left(x+\dfrac{1}{x}\right)=5\Rightarrow\left(x+\dfrac{1}{x}\right)^2=(5)^2$

$\Rightarrow x^2+\dfrac{1}{x^2}+2.x.\dfrac{1}{x}=25$

$\therefore x^2+\dfrac{1}{x^2}=25-2=23.$

$\therefore \left(x^2+\dfrac{1}{x^2}\right)\left(x+\dfrac{1}{x}\right)=23\times5$

$=115$

18. $\because$ $x^2=y+z\Rightarrow x+x^2=x+y+z$
$\Rightarrow x(1+x)=x+y+z$

$y^2=z+x\Rightarrow y+y^2=x+y+z$
$\Rightarrow y(1+y)=x+y+z$
and $z^2=x+y\Rightarrow z+z^2=x+y+z$
$\Rightarrow z(1+z)=x+y+z$
$\therefore$ $x(1+x)=y(1+y)=z(1+z)$
$\qquad =x+y+z=k$

$\therefore x=\dfrac{k}{1+x},y=\dfrac{k}{1+y},z=\dfrac{k}{1+z}$

or $\dfrac{x}{k}=\dfrac{1}{1+x},\dfrac{y}{k}=\dfrac{1}{1+y},$

$\dfrac{z}{k}=\dfrac{1}{1+z}$

$\therefore \dfrac{1}{1+x}+\dfrac{1}{1+y}+\dfrac{1}{1+z}=\dfrac{x}{k}+\dfrac{y}{k}+\dfrac{z}{k}$

$=\dfrac{x+y+z}{k}=\dfrac{k}{k}=1\ [\because x+y+z=k]$

19. $\because$ $a+b+c=0\Rightarrow a+b=-c$
$\therefore$ $(a+b)^2=(-c)^2$
$\Rightarrow a^2+b^2+2ab=c^2$
Similarly, $b^2+c^2-a^2=-2bc$
and $\qquad c^2+a^2-b^2=-2ac$

$\therefore \dfrac{1}{b^2+c^2-a^2}+\dfrac{1}{c^2+a^2-b^2}$

$+\dfrac{1}{a^2+b^2-c^2}$

$=\dfrac{1}{-2bc}+\dfrac{1}{-2ac}+\dfrac{1}{-2ab}$

$=\dfrac{a+b+c}{-2abc}=\dfrac{0}{-2abc}=0$
$\qquad [\because a+b+c=0]$

20. $\because$ $(a+c-b)^2=a^2+c^2+b^2-2ab$
$\qquad\qquad +2ac-2bc$
$\therefore$ $a^2+c^2+b^2-2ab+2ac-2bc$
$=(x+y+2x-1-x+y)^2$
$=(2y+2x-1)^2.$

20

FACTORISATION

1. Factors of $x^2 - 25$ are:
   A. $(x - 1)(x - 25)$
   B. $(x + 25)(x - 1)$
   C. $(x + 5)(x - 5)$
   D. $(x - 5)(x - 5)$

2. Square of $\left(x - \dfrac{1}{x}\right)$ will be
   A. $x^2 - 2 - \dfrac{1}{x^2}$ B. $x^2 - 2 + \dfrac{1}{x^2}$
   C. $x^2 - 4 - \dfrac{1}{x^2}$ D. $x^2 - 2 + \dfrac{1}{x}$

3. Factors of $36 - 9x^2$ will be:
   A. $(6 + 3x)(6 - 3x)$
   B. $(3x - 6)(6 - 3x)$
   C. $(3x + 6)(3x - 6)$
   D. $(12x - 3x)(3 + 3x)$

4. Factors of $8x^3 + y^3$ are:
   A. $(2x + y)(4x^2 - 2xy + y^2)$
   B. $(2x + y)(4x^2 + 2xy + y^2)$
   C. $(2x - y)(4x^2 - 2xy + y^2)$
   D. $(2x + y)(4x^2 - 2xy - y^2)$

5. If the expression $x^3 + 5x^2 - 2 + k$ is completely divisible by $(x - 1)$, the value of k will be:
   A. -3 B. -8
   C. -5 D. -4

6. Find the factors of $x^2 + 3x - 10$
   A. $(x - 1)(x - 10)$
   B. $(x - 2)(x + 5)$
   C. $(x + 2)(x - 5)$
   D. $(x + 2)(x + 5)$

7. Factors of $(x + y)^3 - x - y$ are:
   A. $(x - y)[(x - y)^2 - 1]$
   B. $(x - y)[(x + y)^2 - 1]$
   C. $(x + y)[(x + y)^2 + 1]$
   D. $(x - y)[(x + y)^2 + 1]$

8. Factors of $x^3 y^3 z^3 - 27$ are:
   A. $(xyz - 3)(x^2 y^2 z^2 + 3xyz + 9)$
   B. $(xyz + 3)(x^2 y^2 z^2 + 3xyz + 9)$
   C. $(3 - xyz)(x^2 y^2 z^2 - 3xyz + 9)$
   D. $(xyz - 3)(x^2 y^2 + y^2 z^2 + z^2 x^2)$

9. If $2x - 3 = a$, find the value of $8x^3 - 18ax$
   A. $a^4 + 16$ B. $a^3 + 27$
   C. $a^3 + 64$ D. $a^3 + 125$

10. Factors of $1000 + C^3$ are:
    A. $(10 - c)(100 - 10c + c^2)$
    B. $(10 + c)(100 + 10c + c^2)$
    C. $(10 + c)(100 - 10c + c^2)$
    D. $(10 + c)(100 - 10c - c^2)$

11. If $x = \sqrt{3}$, the value of $x^4 + 2 + \dfrac{1}{x^4}$ will be:
    A. $\dfrac{9}{100}$ B. $\dfrac{81}{100}$
    C. $\dfrac{101}{9}$ D. $\dfrac{100}{9}$

12. Factors of $4x^2 + 8x - 5$ will be:
    A. $(2x - 1)(2x + 5)$
    B. $(2x + 1)(2x + 5)$
    C. $(2x - 5)(2x - 1)$
    D. $(2x + 5)(1 - 2x)$

13. Factors of $a^2 + \dfrac{1}{4} + a$ will be:

A. $\left(a + \dfrac{1}{2}\right)\left(a - \dfrac{1}{2}\right)$ B. $\left(a + \dfrac{1}{2}\right)^2$

C. $\left(a + \dfrac{1}{2}\right)^3$ D. $\left(a + \dfrac{1}{2}\right) \cdot a$

14. What should be added to $(1 + 8x)$ so that the expression obtained may be a perfect square?

A. $8x^2$ B. $9x^2$

C. $16x^2$ D. $25x^2$

15. If $(x - 2)$ is a factor of $x^2 + 2x - a$, the value of a will be:

A. 8 B. 6

C. 11 D. 3

16. Factors of $x^8 + x^4 - 30$ will be:

A. $(x^4 - 5)(x^4 + 6)$
B. $(x^4 + 5)(x^4 - 6)$
C. $(x^4 + 5)(x^4 + 6)$
D. $(x^4 - 10)(x^4 + 3)$

17. Factors of $xy(z^2 + 1) + z(x^2 + y^2)$ will be:

A. $(zx - y)(yz - x)$
B. $(zx + y)(yz + x)$
C. $(xy + z)(yz + x)$
D. $xyz \times (x + y + z)$

18. The value of $\dfrac{789 \times 789 - 211 \times 211}{789 - 211}$ will be:

A. 981 B. 1100

C. 1000 D. 999

ANSWERS

1	2	3	4	5	6	7	8	9	10
C	B	A	A	D	B	B	A	B	C

11	12	13	14	15	16	17	18
D	A	B	C	A	B	B	C

EXPLANATORY ANSWERS

1. $\because x^2 - 25 = (x)^2 - (5)^2$,

[which is of the form $a^2 - b^2$]

$= (x + 5)(x - 5)$.

2. According to question:

Square of $\left(x - \dfrac{1}{x}\right) = \left(x - \dfrac{1}{x}\right)^2$

$= x^2 - 2.x.\dfrac{1}{x} + \left(\dfrac{1}{x}\right)^2 = x^2 - 2 + \dfrac{1}{x^2}$.

3. $\because 36 - 9x^2 = (6)^2 - (3x^2)^2$

[which is of the form $a^2 - b^2$]

$= (6 + 3x)(6 - 3x)$.

4. $\because 8x^3 + y^3 = (2x)^3 + (y)^3$ [which is of the form $a^3 + b^3$]

$= (2x + y)[(2x)^2 - 2x.y + (y)^2]$

$= (2x + y)[4x^2 - 2xy + y^2]$.

5. Since the expression $x^3 + 5x^2 - 2 + k$ is completely divisible by $(x - 1)$

$\therefore$ on substituting $x = 1$ in the given expression, its value will be zero

i.e., $(1)^3 + 5(1)^2 - 2 + k = 0$

$\Rightarrow 1 + 5 - 2 + k = 0$

$\Rightarrow \qquad 4 + k = 0 \Rightarrow k = -4$

Hence value of k is -4.

6. $\because \quad x^2 + 3x - 10 = x^2 + 5x - 2x - 10$

$= x(x + 5) - 2(x + 5) = (x - 2)(x + 5)$

7. $\because (x + y)^3 - x - y = (x + y)^3 - (x + y)$

$= (x + y)[(x + y)^2 - 1]$.

8. $\because$ $x^3y^3z^3 - 27 = (xyz)^3 - (3)^3$

[which is of the form $a^3 - b^3$]

$= (xyz - 3)[(xyz)^2 + xyz.3 + (3)^2]$

$= (xyz - 3)(x^2y^2z^2 + 3xyz + 9)$.

9. $\because$ $2x - 3 = a$

$\Rightarrow \quad 2x = a + 3 \Rightarrow x = \dfrac{a+3}{2}$

$\because$ $8x^3 - 18ax$

$= 8.\left(\dfrac{a+3}{2}\right)^3 - 18a.\left(\dfrac{a+3}{2}\right)$

$= (a+3)^3 - 9a.(a+3)$

$= a^3 + 3.a.3(a+3) + 3^3 - 9a(a+3)$

$= a^3 + 9a(a+3) + 27 - 9a(a+3)$

$= (a^3 + 27)$.

10. $\because$ $1000 + c^3 = (10)^3 + (c)^3$

[which is of the form $a^3 + b^3$]

$= (10 + c)[(10)^2 - 10c + (c)^2]$

$= (10 + c)(100 - 10c + c^2)$.

11. $\because$ $x^4 + 2 + \dfrac{1}{x^4} = (x^2)^2 + 2.x^2.\dfrac{1}{x^2}$

$\qquad + \left(\dfrac{1}{x^2}\right)^2 = \left(x^2 + \dfrac{1}{x^2}\right)^2$

$\therefore$ On substituting $x = \sqrt{3}$

$= \left((\sqrt{3})^2 + \dfrac{1}{(\sqrt{3})^3}\right)^2 = \left(3 + \dfrac{1}{3}\right)^2$

$= \left(\dfrac{10}{3}\right)^2 = \dfrac{100}{9}$.

12. $\because$ $4x^2 + 8x - 5 = 4x^2 + 10x - 2x - 5$

$= 2x(2x + 5) - 1(2x + 5)$

$= (2x - 1)(2x + 5)$.

13. $\because$ $a^2 + \dfrac{1}{4} + a = (a)^2 + 2.\dfrac{1}{2}.a$

$\qquad + \left(\dfrac{1}{2}\right)^2 = \left(a + \dfrac{1}{2}\right)^2$.

14. A trinomial is a perfect square if two of its terms are perfect squares and the third term is equal to twice the product of the square roots of the other two terms. Hence, it is clear that when $16x^2$ is added to $1 + 8x$, the expression obtained is $16x^2 + 8x + 1$, *i.e.*, $(4x)^2 + 2.4x.1 + (1)^2$ which is a perfect square.

15. Since $(x - 2)$ is a factor of $x^2 + 2x - a$

$\therefore$ On substituting $x = 2$ in the expression, the result obtained will be zero

$\therefore$ $(2)^2 + 2.(2) - a = 0$

or $4 + 4 - a = 0$

or $a = 8$

16. $\because$ $x^8 - x^4 - 30 = x^8 - 6x^4 + 5x^4 - 30$

$= x^4(x^4 - 6) + 5(x^4 - 6)$

$= (x^4 + 5)(x^4 - 6)$.

17. $\because$ $xy(z^2 + 1) + z(x^2 + y^2)$

$= xyz^2 + xy + zx^2 + y^2z$

$= (xyz^2 + zx^2) + y^2z + xy$

$= zx(yz + x) + y(yz + x)$

$= (zx + y)(yz + x)$.

18. Suppose $789 = a$, $211 = b$

$\therefore$ $\dfrac{789 \times 789 - 211 \times 211}{789 - 211}$

$= \dfrac{a^2 - b^2}{a - b} = \dfrac{(a+b)(a-b)}{a-b}$

$= a + b$

On substituting the value of a and b

$\therefore$ $a + b = 789 + 211 = 1000$.

21

PROBLEMS ON NUMBERS

1. The difference of two numbers is 5 and the difference of their squares is 135. The sum of the numbers is:
   A. 27   B. 25
   C. 30   D. 32

2. The sum of two numbers is 29 and the difference of their squares is 145. The difference between the numbers is:
   A. 13   B. 5
   C. 8   D. 11

3. The difference of two numbers is 8 and $\frac{1}{8}$ th of their sum is 35. The numbers are:
   A. 132, 140   B. 128, 136
   C. 124, 132   D. 136, 144

4. The sum of two numbers is 100 and their difference is 37. The difference of their squares is:
   A. 37   B. 100
   C. 63   D. 3700

5. The ratio between two numbers is 3 : 4 and their sum is 420. The greater of the two numbers is:
   A. 175   B. 200
   C. 240   D. 315

6. The difference between the squares of two consecutive numbers is 35. The numbers are:
   A. 14, 15   B. 15, 16
   C. 17, 18   D. 18, 19

7. Three fourth of one-fifth of a number is 60. The number is:
   A. 300   B. 400
   C. 450   D. 1200

8. A number is 45 more than its two-fifth. The number is:
   A. 60   B. 80
   C. $\frac{125}{3}$ D. $\frac{125}{7}$

9. 24 is divided into two parts such that 7 times the first part added to 5 times the second part makes 146. The first part is:
   A. 11   B. 13
   C. 16   D. 17

10. If one-fifth of a number decreased by 5 is 5, then the number is:
    A. 25   B. 50
    C. 60   D. 75

11. $\frac{1}{4}$ of a number subtracted from $\frac{1}{3}$ of the number gives 12. The number is:
    A. 144   B. 120
    C. 72   D. 63

12. $\frac{3}{4}$ of a number is 19 less than the original number. The number is:
    A. 84   B. 64
    C. 76   D. 72

13. A number is as much greater than 31 as is less than 55. The number is:

A. 47   B. 52
C. 39   D. 43

14. 11 times a number gives 132. The number is:

A. 11
B. 12
C. 13.2
D. None of these

15. Three-fourth of a number is more than two-third of the number by 5. The number is:

A. 72   B. 60
C. 84   D. 48

16. $\dfrac{4}{5}$ of a certain number is 64. Half of that number is:

A. 32   B. 40
C. 80   D. 16

17. A positive number when decreased by 4, is equal to 21 times the reciprocal of the number. The number is:

A. 3   B. 5
C. 7   D. 9

18. The sum of two numbers is 15 and sum of their squares is 113. the numbers are:

A. 4, 11   B. 5, 10
C. 6, 9   D. 7, 8

19. The sum of two numbers is twice their difference. If one of the numbers is 10, the other number is:

A. $3\dfrac{1}{3}$ B. 30

C. $-3\dfrac{1}{3}$ D. $4\dfrac{1}{4}$

20. The sum of squares of two numbers is 80 and the square of their difference is 36. The product of the two numbers is:

A. 22   B. 44
C. 58   D. 116

21. The product of two numbers is 120. The sum of their squares is 289. The sum of the two numbers is:

A. 20
B. 23
C. 169
D. None of these

22. A number whose fifth part increased by 5 is equal to its fourth part diminshed by 5, is:

A. 160   B. 180
C. 200   D. 220

23. If one-fourth of one-third of one-half of a number is 15, the number is:

A. 72   B. 120
C. 180   D. 360

24. $\dfrac{4}{5}$ of a number exceeds its $\dfrac{2}{3}$ by 8. The number is:

A. 30
B. 60
C. 90
D. None of these

25. If 1 is added to the denominator of a fraction, the fraction becomes $\dfrac{1}{2}$. If 1 is added to the numerator, the fraction becomes 1. The fraction is:

A. $\dfrac{4}{7}$ B. $\dfrac{5}{9}$

C. $\dfrac{2}{3}$ D. $\dfrac{10}{11}$

ANSWERS

1	2	3	4	5	6	7	8	9	10
A	B	D	D	C	C	B	C	B	B

11	12	13	14	15	16	17	18	19	20
A	C	D	B	B	B	C	D	B	A

21	22	23	24	25
B	C	D	B	C

EXPLANATORY ANSWERS

1. Let the numbers be a and b

Then, $(a + b) = \dfrac{(a^2 - b^2)}{(a - b)}$

$$= \dfrac{135}{5} = 27.$$

2. Let the numbers be a and b

Then, $(a - b) = \dfrac{(a^2 - b^2)}{(a + b)}$

$$= \dfrac{145}{29} = 5.$$

3. Let the numbers be x and $(x + 8)$

Then, $\dfrac{1}{8}[x + (x + 8)] = 35$

or $2x + 8 = 280$

or $\quad 2x = 272$ or $x = 136.$

4. Let the numbers be a and b
Then, $a + b = 100$ and $a - b = 37$
$\therefore a^2 - b^2 = (a + b)(a - b)$
$$= 100 \times 37 = 3700.$$

5. Let the numbers be $3x$ and $4x$
Then, $3x + 4x = 420$
$\Rightarrow 7x = 420 \Rightarrow x = 60$
$\therefore$ Greater number $= 4 \times 60 = 240.$

6. Let the numbers be x and $(x + 1)$
Then, $(x + 1)^2 - x^2 = 35$

$\Rightarrow x^2 + 2x + 1 - x^2 = 35$
$\Rightarrow 2x = 34$ or $x = 17$
So, the numbers are 17 and 18.

7. Let the number be x. Then,
$$\dfrac{3}{4} \times \dfrac{1}{5} \times x = 60$$
$\Rightarrow 3x = 1200$ or $x = 400.$
So, the numbers are 136 and 144.

8. Let the number be x. Then,
$$x - 25 = \dfrac{2}{5}x \quad \text{or } 5x - 125 = 2x$$
or $\quad x = \dfrac{125}{3}$

9. Let the first part be x and 2nd part be $(24 - x)$
Then,
$7x + 5(24 - x) = 146$
$\Rightarrow 7x + 120 - 5x = 146$
$\Rightarrow 2x = 26$ or $x = 13.$
$\therefore$ First part $= 13.$

10. Let the number be x. Then,
$$\dfrac{x}{5} - 5 = 5 \Rightarrow \dfrac{x}{5} = 10 \Rightarrow x = 50.$$

11. Let the number be x. Then,
$$\dfrac{x}{3} - \dfrac{x}{4} = 12 \Rightarrow \dfrac{4x - 3x}{12} = 12$$
$\Rightarrow x = 144.$

12. Let the original number be x. Then,

$$\frac{3}{4}x + 19 = x \Rightarrow 3x + 76 = 4x$$

$$\Rightarrow x = 76.$$

13. Let the number be x. Then,

$$x - 31 = 55 - x$$
$$\Rightarrow 2x = 55 + 31 = 86$$
or $x = 43.$

14. Let the number be x.
Then, $11x = 132 \Rightarrow x = 12.$

15. Let the number be x. Then,

$$\frac{3}{4}x - \frac{2}{3}x = 5 \Rightarrow \frac{9x - 8x}{12} = 5$$

$$\Rightarrow \qquad x = 60.$$

16. Let the number be x. Then,

$$\frac{4}{5}x = 64 \Rightarrow x = \frac{64 \times 5}{4} = 80.$$

$\therefore$ Half of the number $= 40.$

17. Let the number be x. Then,

$$x - 4 = \frac{21}{x} \Rightarrow x^2 - 4x - 21 = 0$$

$$\Rightarrow x^2 - 7x + 3x - 21 = 0$$
$$\Rightarrow x(x - 7) + 3(x - 7) = 0$$
$$\Rightarrow (x - 7)(x + 37) = 0$$
$$\Rightarrow x = 7$$

(neglecting $x = -3$)

18. Let the numbers be x and $(15 - x)$
Then, $x^2 + (15 - x)^2 = 113$
or $x^2 - 15x + 56 = 0$
$\therefore$ $x = 8$ or $x = 7.$
So, the numbers are 7, 8.

19. Let the other number be x.
Then, $10 + x = 2 (x - 10)$
$$\Rightarrow \qquad x = 30.$$

20. Let the numbers be a and b. Then,

$a^2 + b^2 = 80$ and $(a - b)^2 = 36$
$(a - b)^2 = 36$
$$\Rightarrow a^2 + b^2 - 2ab = 36$$
$$\Rightarrow 2ab = (a^2 + b^2) - 36$$
$$= 80 - 36 = 44$$
$$\Rightarrow ab = 22.$$

21. Let the numbers be a and b. Then,
$(a + b)^2 = (a^2 + b^2) + 2ab$
$$= 289 + 2 \times 120$$
$$= 289 + 240 = 529$$

$\therefore a + b = \sqrt{529} = 23.$

22. Let the number be x. Then,

$$\frac{x}{5} + 5 = \frac{x}{4} - 5 \Rightarrow \frac{x}{4} - \frac{x}{5} = 10$$

or $\dfrac{5x - 4x}{20} = 10$

$$\Rightarrow \qquad x = 200.$$

23. Let the number be x. Then,

$$\frac{1}{4} \text{ of } \frac{1}{3} \text{ of } \frac{1}{2} \text{ of } x = 15$$

$$\frac{1}{24}x = 15 \Rightarrow x = 24 \times 15 = 360.$$

24. Let the number be x. Then,

$$\frac{4}{5}x - \frac{2}{3}x = 8 \Rightarrow \frac{12x - 10x}{15} = 8$$

$$\Rightarrow 2x = 120 \text{ or } x = 60.$$

25. Let the required fraction be $\dfrac{x}{y}$.

Then,

$$\frac{x}{y + 1} = \frac{1}{2} \Rightarrow 2x - y = 1$$

and $\dfrac{x + 1}{y} = 1 \Rightarrow x - y = -1.$

Solving $2x - y = 1$ and $x - y = -1$,
we get $x = 2, y = 3.$

$\therefore$ The fraction is $\dfrac{2}{3}.$

22

MISCELLANEOUS

1. The value of $(1502)^2 - (1498)^2$ is
   A. 12,000
   B. 16,000
   C. 22,56,004
   D. 22,560

2. $\sqrt[3]{1 - \dfrac{91}{216}}$ is equal to

   A. $\dfrac{1}{6}$

   B. $\dfrac{5}{6}$

   C. $1 - \dfrac{\sqrt[3]{91}}{6}$

   D. None of these

3. A number exceeds its four seventh by 18. What is number?
   A. 36
   B. 49
   C. 63
   D. None of these

4. The highest common factor of 70 and 245 is:
   A. 35
   B. 55
   C. 45
   D. 65

5. If 5 poles are erected at equal distances between two points 20 metres apart, what is the distance between any two poles?
   A. 2 metres
   B. 3 metres
   C. 4 metres
   D. 5 metres

6. The difference of two numbers is 11 and $\dfrac{1}{5}$ th of their sum is 9. The numbers are:
   A. 31, 20
   B. 30, 19
   C. 29, 18
   D. 28, 17

7. Two consecutive muliples of a certain number add upto 184. The number is
   A. 4
   B. 8
   C. 23
   D. 46

8. The smallest number, which must be added to 1000 to make it a perfect square, is:
   A. 12
   B. 20
   C. 24
   D. 25

9. The least square number exactly divisible by 8, 12, 15 and 20, is:
   A. 900
   B. 1200
   C. 3600
   D. 14400

10. In an examination, 35% of the total students failed in Hindi, 45% failed in English and 20% in both. Percentage of total students passed in both the subjects is:
    A. 10
    B. 20
    C. 30
    D. 40

11. The sum of any seven consecutive whole numbers is always divisible by
    A. 2
    B. 3
    C. 7
    D. 11

12. The sum of two numbers is 104 and their difference is 30. The difference of their squares is:

A. 74   B. 2160
C. 2320   D. 3120

13. 10% of 24.2 will be how much more than 10% of 24.02?

A. 0.02   B. 0.18
C. 0.018   D. 0.002

14. A trader lists his articles 20% above C.P. and allows a discount of 10% on cash payment. His gain percent is:

A. 5%   B. 6%
C. 8%   D. 10%

15. Two different natural numbers are such that their product is less than their sum. One of the numbers must be

A. 1
B. 2
C. 3
D. None of these

16. At an election involving two condidates, only 68 votes are declared as invalid. The winning condidate scores 52% and wins by 98 votes. The total number of votes polled is:

A. 2382   B. 2450
C. 2518   D. 750

17. Deepak has ₹ 5130 in the form of 1, 2 and 5 rupee notes. If these notes be in the ratio 3 : 7 : 8, the number of five rupee notes he has is:

A. 340   B. 672
C. 720   D. 768

18. The compound interest on ₹ 6000 for $1\frac{1}{2}$ years at 10% per annum, the interest being paid half yearly, will be:

A. ₹ 912.75   B. ₹ 930
C. ₹ 932.50   D. ₹ 945.75

19. Jayant started a business investing ₹ 6000. Six months later Madhu joined him investing ₹ 4000. If they make a profit of ₹ 5200 at the end of the year, how much should be the share of Madhu?

A. ₹ 1300   B. ₹ 1732
C. ₹ 3466   D. ₹ 3900

20. ₹ 1200 amounts to ₹ 1632 in four years at a certain rate of simple interest. If the rate of interest is increased by 1%, it would amount to how much?

A. ₹ 1635   B. ₹ 1644
C. ₹ 1670   D. ₹ 1680

ANSWERS

1	2	3	4	5	6	7	8	9	10
A	B	D	A	D	D	B	C	C	D

11	12	13	14	15	16	17	18	19	20
C	D	C	C	A	D	C	D	A	D

EXPLANATORY ANSWERS

1. $(1502)^2 - (1498)^2$
$= (1502 - 1498)(1502 + 1498)$
$= 4 \times 3000 = 12000.$

2. $\sqrt[3]{1 - \dfrac{91}{216}} = \left(\dfrac{216 - 91}{216}\right)^{1/3}$

$= \left(\dfrac{125}{216}\right)^{1/3} = \left(\dfrac{5 \times 5 \times 5}{6 \times 6 \times 6}\right)^{1/.3}$

$= \dfrac{5}{6}.$

3. $x - \dfrac{4}{7}x = 18 \implies 7x - 4x = 126$
or $x = 42.$

4.
```
   70)245(3
      210
      ───
      35)70(2
         70
         ──
          ×
         ──
```
$\therefore$ H.C.F. = 35.

5. Distance between two poles
$= \dfrac{20}{(5-1)} = 5$ metres.

6. Let the numbers be x and $x - 11.$
$\dfrac{1}{5}(x + x - 11) = 9$
or $\quad 2x - 11 = 45$ or $x = 28$
$\therefore$ The numbers are 28, 17.

7. $184 = 2 \times 2 \times 2 \times 23$
$mx + m(x + 1) = 184$
So, $m[2x + 1] = 184$
or $\quad 2x + 1 = \dfrac{184}{m}$
By hit and trial, $m = 8$ and $x = 11.$
So, the number = 8.

8.
```
 3 | 1000(31
   |    9
   |    ───
61 |  100
   |   61
   |  ───
   |   39
```
Number to be added
$= (32)^2 - 1000$
$= (1024 - 1000) = 24.$

9. L.C.M. of 8, 12, 15, 20
$= 2 \times 3 \times 2 \times 5 \times 2$
$\therefore$ Leaset square number divisible
by 8, 12, 15, 20
$= 2 \times 2 \times 3 \times 3 \times 5 \times 5 \times 2 \times 2$
$= 3600.$

10. Failed in Hindi only
$= (35 - 20) = 15\%$
Failed in English only
$= (45 - 20) = 25\%$
Failed in both = 20%
Failed in one or both
$= (1\ 5 + 25 + 20)\% = 60\%$
Passed in both = 40%.

11. $1 + 2 + 3 + 4 + 5 + 6 + 7 = 28,$
which is divisible by 7.

12. $x + y = 104$ and $x - y = 30$
$\therefore (x^2 - y^2) = (x + y)(x - y)$
$= 104 \times 30 = 3120.$

13. It is more by
$\left(\dfrac{10}{100} \times 24.2 - \dfrac{10}{100} \times 24.02\right)$
$= 2.42 - 2.402 = 0.018.$

14. Let C.P. = ₹ 100.
Then, list price = ₹ 120.
S.P. = 90% of ₹ 120 = ₹ 108.
Gain = 8%.

15. Clearly, $1x < 1 + x$.
So, one of the numbers must be 1.

16. Let total votes polled = x. Then,
52% of x + (52% of x − 98) + 68 = x

$$2 \times \frac{52}{100} \, x - x = 30$$

or $x = (30 \times 25) = 750$.

17. Let these notes be $3x$, $7x$ and $8x$.
Ratio of their values
$$= 3x \times 1 : 7x \times 2 : 8x \times 5$$
$$= 3x : 14x : 40x$$
$$= 3 : 14 : 40.$$
Value of 5 rupee notes
$$= ₹\left(5130 \times \frac{40}{57} \right) = ₹\, 3600$$

Number of these notes $= \dfrac{3600}{5}$
$$= 720.$$

18. C.I. $= ₹\left[6000 \times \left(1 + \dfrac{5}{100} \right)^3 - 6000 \right]$

$= ₹\left[6000 \times \dfrac{21}{20} \times \dfrac{21}{20} \times \dfrac{21}{20} - 6000 \right]$

$= ₹\, 945.75.$

19. Jayant : Madhu = (6000 × 12 : 4000 × 6) = 3 : 1.

Madhu's share $= ₹\left(5200 \times \dfrac{1}{4} \right)$
$$= ₹\, 1300.$$

20. Rate $= \dfrac{100 \times 432}{1200 \times 4} = 9\%.$
New rate = 10%

New interest $= ₹\left(\dfrac{1200 \times 10 \times 4}{100} \right)$
$$= ₹\, 480$$
Amount $= ₹\, 1680.$